EATING CLOSE TO HOME

Happy Birthday, Kristyn!

Elin England

EATING CLOSE TO HOME

A GUIDE TO LOCAL
SEASONAL SUSTENANCE
IN THE PACIFIC NORTHWEST

ELIN KRISTINA ENGLAND

2008/2009 EDITION

Elin would love to know your ideas about eating close to home.
You can reach her at elkdream_farm@yahoo.com

Eating Close to Home / January 2009
All rights reserved.
Copyright © 2009 by Elin Kristina England.
Author photo by Kyra Schneider.
Front cover and page design by Gray Design.
Production design and copy editing by Lynn Marx.

ISBN 978-0-578-00069-5

ABOUT THIS BOOK

Some years ago, before Local Food became a popular refrain, back when sustainability was not a marketing ploy—so far back, indeed, that Peak Oil was still a new topic, I was engaged in a discussion with my husband about the question of whether people living in Lane County, Oregon, could feed themselves solely on food grown and processed in this watershed. It is possible, he said, according to a study that had just been completed by what is now the Willamette Farm & Food Coalition. Assuming, he added, that people would be willing to eat less beef and more seasonal vegetables. Which is a great idea, I countered, and we could move in that direction, except that most folks have forgotten what to do with winter vegetables such as parsnips and rutabagas. In order to encourage people to give up on the idea that they need zucchini and head lettuce twelve months of the year, I suggested, someone should write a cookbook.

Right, he said, waggling his eyebrows at me. Someone should.

So I took the hint and set about writing a cookbook. It wasn't such an odd idea, really. I have long been inclined to eat seasonally, a habit begun, no doubt, by my mother, who, when I was young, steadfastly refused all requests to buy peaches and strawberries, until they were in season. Childhood summers on Nantucket included feasts of bluefish—when they were running—pulled out of the ocean and deposited almost directly on the grill, and pies from freshly picked wild blueberries—if we made it down to the island in time for berry season. As a mother and a gardener, I tend now to cook largely from what is available in the garden and orchard, both in order to consume the bounty that our piece of earth provides, and in order to keep the economy of our household in good order.

Nonetheless, despite being a devout book worm, a fairly obsessed gardener, and quite comfortable in the kitchen, the idea of creating my own cookbook was a bit daunting. So I began, as I begin most projects, by reading other books. I pulled Joan Dye Gussow's book off the shelf and re-read it. I found Brian Halweil's writings, Frances Moore Lappé's recent book, and many pieces by Michael Pollan. I scoured the internet. I read and cooked and organized my recipes and read some more, and after a bit I began to write. And all the while (because I was not just writing, of course, I was also mothering and working and gardening and dealing with medical crises), *other* people were also starting to think more about the need to eat locally and tread lightly on our earth, and they started writing *their* books too. So by the time this book began to feel less like a pipe-dream and more like what you might consider a manuscript, the local food movement was not only born, but up and walking on two legs and trailing behind it was a very respectable bibliography.

A great many of you who read this book may find that you've heard it all before — how America has divorced itself from the sources of its sustenance. How the act of putting a meal on the table can be considered one of the more destructive acts that we regularly wreak on our fragile biosphere. How if we don't start paying attention to where our food comes from and how it is grown and re-learn how to feed ourselves, we may find ourselves sitting down to empty tables.

Others have written very eloquently and persuasively about these issues, and I hope you will read their books. My favorites are listed in the back. But if you are new to the idea that we need to relocalize our economies, support our local farmers, and re-examine our shopping lists, then I hope you will take a few minutes to read the first part this book. And even if you have recently read Barbara Kingsolver and Jane Goodall and Michael Abelman and Gary Paul Nabhan, I hope this collection of recipes will encourage you to learn to live and eat happily with the foods that are grown nearby, in the seasons that they are available.

And this is just the beginning! Please, don't take this as anything close to the final word on what to do with all those strange winter vegetables or how to process boatloads of tomatoes. Create your own recipes. Collect ideas from your friends. Talk to your farmer! Consult many recipe books. Search the internet. There are new books on eating seasonally being written all the time and new websites popping up almost daily. And then share that information! If we are going to change the way we do business, if we are going to save this planet and all of the many species dependant on its resources, we must work together. We are all connected.

Bon Appétit!

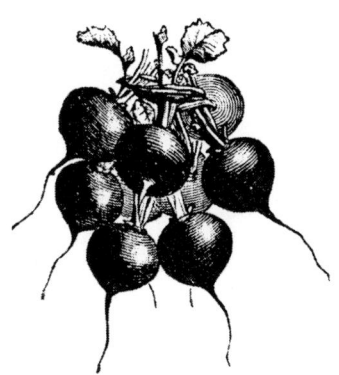

GIVE THANKS

So many threads have interwoven to create the tapestry of my life, and so many more will continue to do so. Friends, family, teachers and healers. I give thanks to each and every one of you. A few, however, must be called out by name:

My husband, Don, the true love of my life, kindred spirit, ever present strength. This book would not have come into existence without you.

My children, Kyra and Kory. What excellent teachers you are.

My mother, Joanna, who instilled in me a great love of food and zest for trying new recipes. And my father, Carl, who found them all to be Very Tasty.

Farmor, my father's mother, who waits for me, on the other side, ready to put down her book and join me for a cup of tea and a Pilot cracker spread with cream cheese and black currant jam.

Lynn Marx, my production designer, who massaged the manuscript into shape and, like a true midwife, saw it through the last stages of delivery.

Finally, I give thanks to those who have gone before, on whose strong backs we have climbed, whose work-calloused hands support us still, and whose wind- and sun-creased faces beam love and encouragement at us as we seek to re-emerge. And for those who will come after—we do this for you.

CONTENTS

EATING CLOSE TO HOME | 15

THE SEASONS, WHAT IS AVAILABLE, WHAT TO DO WITH IT | 33
    Fruit and Vegetable Availability Chart | 34

WINTER • December • January • February | 37

WINTER NIBBLES
    White Bean Dip | 43
    Pesto Log | 44
    Claudia's Mushroom Crostini | 45

WINTER SALADS
    Kale Salad | 46
    Unbelievably Good Coleslaw | 47
    Cabbage and Apple Salad | 48
    Wintergreen Farm Cabbage Slaw | 49

WINTER SOUPS
    Bean Soup Mix | 50
    Mighty Fine Bean Soup | 51
    Curried Winter Vegetable Soup | 52
    Mom's Favorite Salmon Chowder | 53
    Salmon and Corn Chowder | 54
    Carrot Ginger Soup | 55

WINTER MAIN DISHES
    Curried Tofu and Vegetables | 56
    Joanna's Beef Stew | 58
    Bulgar and Winter Vegetables | 59

Stifado | 60

Winter Vegetable Gratin | 61

Chicken Pot Pie | 62

English Shepherd's Pie | 64

Pasta with Sausages and Greens | 65

WINTER SIDE DISHES

The Mid-Winter Vegetable Cure | 66

Mashed Rutabaga | 67

Potarrots | 67

Cauliflower with Cumin and Cheese | 68

Dave's Savory Collard Greens | 69

Farm-Style Braised Kale | 70

Roasted Parsnips | 70

Carrots with Ginger and Cardamom | 71

Carrot and Turnip Pancakes | 72

Sri Lankan Cabbage | 73

Celeriac and Potato Purée | 74

Spicy Red Cabbage | 75

Winter Squash with Cider Glaze and Sage Butter | 76

WINTER BAKED GOODS AND TASTY TREATS

Sunday Morning Muffins | 77

Baked Breakfast Pudding | 78

Frozen Berry Crisp | 79

Mixed Fruit Compote | 80

Baked Apples with Lingonberries | 81

SPRING • March • April • May | 83

SPRING NIBBLES

Fava Bean Crostini | 88

Tofu Paté with Spring Herbs | 89

SPRING SALADS

    The Ultimate Tossed Green Salad | 90
    Elin's Favorite Salad Dressing | 91
    Beet and Arugula Salad with Fresh Chèvre | 91
    Fava Bean Salad | 92
    Baby Beet Salad | 93
    Wheat Berry Salad with Fresh Peas | 94

SPRING SOUPS

    Cream of Asparagus Soup | 95
    Potato Leek Soup | 96

SPRING MAIN DISHES

    Green Rice | 97
    Asparagus with Mushrooms and Rice | 98
    Spring Frittata | 100
    Lentils with Butter and Parsley | 101
    Northwest Noodles | 102
    Pasta with Kale "Rabe" and Tuna | 103
    Jake's Tofu-Turkey Pie | 104

SPRING SIDE DISHES

    Spinach with Sesame Dressing | 105
    Ginger-Marinated Asparagus | 106
    Kohlrabi Fritters with Fresh Herbs | 107
    Roast Beets with Thyme and Garlic | 108

SPRING BAKED GOODS AND TASTY TREATS

    Rhubarb Crisp | 109
    Rhubarb Sauce | 110
    Marijo's Rhubarb Cake | 111

SUMMER • June • July • August | 113

SUMMER NIBBLES
   Claudia's Summer Crostini | 118
   Eggplant Bruschetta | 119
   Bill Mumbach's Fresh Sweet Onion Rings with Basil | 120

SUMMER SALADS
   Tomatoes Lutèce | 121
   Pasta Salad with Tomato and Feta Cheese | 122
   Farmor's Potato Salad | 123
   Natasha's Venezuelan Boyfriend's Aunt's Green Salad | 124
   Tabbouli | 125

SUMMER SOUPS
   Gazpacho | 126

SUMMER MAIN DISHES
   Baked Tomato Spaghetti | 127
   Red Devil Squash Creole | 128
   Pad Thai | 129
   Asian-Style Honey Glazed Ribs | 130
   Groundwork Organics Favorite Veggie Melt | 131
   Mexican Veggie Pot Pie | 132
   Good Corn Bread | 133

SUMMER SIDE DISHES
   Stillpoint Farm's Grilled Japanese Eggplant | 134
   Mexican Corn | 134
   Risotto with Onions, Carrots and Fennel | 135
   Green Bean Tomato Curry | 136
   Sage-Roasted Summer Squash | 137
   Oil-Roasted Green Beans, Potatoes and Fennel 137

SUMMER BAKED GOODS AND TASTY TREATS
    Berry Good Sauce | 138
    Blackberry Cobbler | 139

FALL • September • October • November | *141*

FALL NIBBLES
    Kinpira | 145
    Dried Tomato Pesto | 146

FALL SALADS
    Bartlett Pear Salad | 147
    Kohlrabi and Sungold Tomato Salad | 148
    Raw Beet Salad | 148
    Coleslaw with Ginger-Mustard Dressing | 149
    Kohlrabi and Carrot Salad | 150

FALL SOUPS
    Barley and Lentil Soup with Swiss Chard | 151
    Minestrone | 152
    The Real Deal Cream of Tomato Soup | 154

FALL MAIN DISHES
    Swiss Chard with Currants and Walnuts | 155
    Calzone | 156
    Potato and Chard Bake | 157
    White Bean, Squash, Kale and Olive Stew | 158
    Sally's Favorite Sausage and Peppers | 159
    Chard and Potato Enchiladas | 160
    Home-Made Enchilada Sauce | 161
    Tempato Patties | 162
    Cranberry Sauce for Grilled or Poached Salmon | 163

Blackberry Sauce for Salmon | 164

Peder's Favorite Salmon Marinade | 164

Fall Stew | 165

Ratatouille with Polenta | 166

Polenta with Greens | 168

FALL SIDE DISHES

Sesame Soy Braised Bok Choi | 169

Squash Pancakes | 170

Fried Green Tomatoes | 171

Roast Roots | 172

Squished Squash | 173

Stuffed Squash | 174

Lemon-Garlic Broccoli | 175

FALL BAKED GOODS AND TASTY TREATS

Hazelnut Buttermilk Pancakes | 176

Ginger Baked Apples | 177

Blackberry Butter | 177

Fresh Pear/Apple Crumble Pie | 178

Pear Crisp | 179

Apple Pie with Sage | 180

DISHES TO FIT ANY SEASON | 183

Pizza Crust | 184

The Kid's Favorite Pizza | 185

Pesto Pizza | 185

Zucchini and Basil Pizza | 186

Pesto and Fresh Tomato Pizza | 186

Pizza with Greens | 187

PUTTING FOOD BY | *189*
    Roasted Tomato Sauce | *192*
    Debbie's Roasted Tomato Sauce | *193*
    Basil Pesto | *196*
    Cilantro Parsley Pesto | *197*
    Dilly Pesto | *197*
    Roasted Peppers from Stillpoint Farm | *198*
    Dilly Beans | *199*
    Aunt Stel's Piccalilli | *200*
    Lars Watson's Mother's Famous Bread and Butter Pickles | *201*
    Joanna's Caramel Spice Pear Butter | *202*

GOING MORE LOCAL | *205*
    Our Favorite Granola | *206*
    Whole Grain Salads | *207*
    Beans, Greens & Grains | *208*

REFERENCES | *213*

CONTRIBUTORS | *216*

LOCAL RESOURCES | *218*

HELPFUL WEBSITES | *220*

INDEX | *222*

The industrial eater is, in fact, one who does not
know that eating is an agricultural act,
who no longer knows or imagines the connections
between eating and the land, and who
is therefore necessarily passive and uncritical...

We still (sometimes) remember that
we cannot be free if our minds and voices
are controlled by someone else.

But we have neglected to understand that
we cannot be free if our food and its sources are
controlled by someone else.

The condition of the passive consumer of food
is not a democratic condition.

One reason to eat responsibly is to live free.

—Wendell Berry, *The Pleasures of Eating*

EATING CLOSE TO HOME

There was a time when we all, of necessity, ate closer to home. Milk came from the local dairy; wheat was grown in nearby fields and ground into flour at the local mill. Cattle, hogs and chickens lived on nearby farms, and produce at the local green grocer was limited to what was grown in local fields.

Today, thanks to the wonders of GMOs, plastic wrap, refrigeration, preservatives, and, until recently, inexpensive fuel, the milk we pour on our cereal may have come from cows grazing in fields many day's drive from where we live, and fed on grain from yet another region — or country! Our bread may well be made from wheat grown in one state, ground in another, and baked in a third before ending up in our shopping cart. Most of our meat and eggs come from feedlots and factories located hundreds, if not thousands, of miles from our neighborhood grocery store. And the grapes on our plate may have been grown in another hemisphere. In fact, at the time of this writing, local food accounts for only 1% of the $900 billion food industry.

Is it any wonder that food just doesn't taste like it used to — or like we are told it used to taste?

We have become a nation of consumers with little connection to the food that sustains us. We buy asparagus for a dinner party in January, because it is there in the grocery store at an unsustainably low price per pound, with little regard for where in the world asparagus is in season in January and what the true cost to the environment is to get it from there to here. We buy peaches in March "because they look so good!" and are disappointed — again — that they have but a fraction of the flavor (much less the nutritional value) of a tree-ripened peach. And we seem to have collectively succumbed to the myth that a green lettuce salad with a tomato should be part of every dinner from January to December.

Food that has been raised locally and brought to your table fresh from the farm is full of flavor, high in nutrition, and low in preservatives. It has often been raised organically as well, leaving it free of pesticide and herbicide residue. Eating close to home also benefits your community; when you purchase food grown by local farmers, the money you pay stays in your community, rather than profiting the shareholders of a mega-corporation that is probably not based in your state—or even your country. A locally based diet is good for our country and good for the world. It is an ironic fact that the world-wide production of the food that gives us sustenance is one of the largest businesses, and also arguably one of the worst destroyers of our land. The vast amounts of petrochemicals used to plant, fertilize, harvest, process and ship our food are poisoning our planet, and will, as oil prices continue to skyrocket and supplies dwindle, become increasingly untenable. Our dependence, as a country, on food that has been grown on the other side of the globe, leaves us lacking in food security.

But there is another way! It is possible to eat food that is grown locally and harvested in season year round. It does mean changing our habits and rearranging our thinking a bit. It also requires a little more effort in the kitchen—but with very tasty results! In this book I will speak first about the reasons to eat closer to home, to give you some incentive to change your habits. Then I will take you through the seasons, and help you find ways to cook local, seasonal foods. I am writing from the perspective of the Pacific Northwest, since that is where I live and cook and garden. I know the rhythm of the seasons here, and when various foods are ready to be rushed from garden to table, brimming with flavor and nutrition. If you are reading this book in Alabama, you might not be eating frost-sweetened Brussels sprouts in November… and you are likely eating tomatoes a lot earlier than we will on the West Coast! The timing will be different in different regions, but the reasons for eating locally grown foods are the same.

WHAT DOES IT MEAN?

Eating close to home involves several things. It involves eating locally grown and produced foods. It encourages you to eat foods that are in season. It inspires eating more meals made from scratch and fewer from a box. And it can mean choosing restaurants that support local food producers and whose menus focus on seasonal foods.

Locally grown food is not limited to fresh fruits and vegetables, although those may be the first items that come to mind when you contemplate relocalizing your shopping. There are probably farmers near you who raise cattle, poultry, pigs and lamb. There may be fish markets where you can ask which fish came from local waters. Farmers markets often have vendors who sell hand-made cheeses, locally grown nuts, and jams, jellies and syrups made from berries harvested in your area. Consider buying bread from a local bakery rather than a loaf of double-wrapped bread baked on the other side of the continent.

Eating food when it is in season becomes more natural when you focus on buying produce that has been raised locally. This is relatively easy to do in the summer when produce stands selling fresh corn, tomatoes, zucchini and melons pop up like weeds after a summer rain shower. More challenging is eating seasonal food in the winter and early spring, when fresh produce is largely limited to stored root vegetables and over-wintering greens. This is the time to call into play tomatoes picked fresh and dried or canned in August, as well as the frozen berries, peaches, vegetables and herbs that you have put by to add a taste of summer when the skies are gray.

Eating locally grown foods also entails eating fewer processed foods. Unless you live near one of the large multi-national food processing facilities (and perhaps not even then), most of the crackers, cookies and snack foods available in your local grocery store are anything but local. Frozen pre-cooked dinners are certainly made from ingredients purchased from far and wide. Perhaps it is not realistic to cut processed food out of your pantry completely—particularly if you have kids in the house. But you can limit what you buy, and get in the habit of serving fresher, more nutritious alternatives. Happily, food that has not spent weeks in a warehouse has more flavor.

When produce goes directly from the farm to your table it is so full of flavor that it can be prepared simply and still delight the palate. Intricate sauces and expensive imported seasonings are not as necessary, so cooking is easier, less expensive and less time consuming.

Many Americans eat at restaurants several times a week. Most restaurants do not serve locally grown foods or focus on foods that are in season. But there is a growing trend toward restaurants that do utilize organic and local foods. Encourage this trend by asking your server which foods on the menu are grown locally. Suggest that you would be interested in a menu that features seasonal foods. Chances are, if your chef knows there is an interest, he or she will be more inclined to add those items to the menu.

WHY EAT CLOSE TO HOME?

It is hard to make big changes in lifestyle. We are comfortable with old patterns; it takes a lot to jolt us out of them. Until recently, there was no great financial incentive to eat local and seasonal foods. However, as the world's oil reserves dwindle, the cost of the ubiquitous tossed green salad with cucumber and tomato in the middle of winter in the Northeast is becoming prohibitive for many people, making creative winter slaws an obvious choice. Hopefully, an increasing number of people will realize that if you add the true cost to the planet to the price of a cantaloupe shipped from Chile, it will be clear that waiting a few months for locally raised melons is the more cost effective choice.

Historically, organically grown food has cost more than conventional, and locally raised food has been more expensive as well. The small farmers who grow those beautiful lettuces you see in the farmers market do not have the economies of scale to sell their produce to you for a fraction of what it really costs to grow it, nor do they receive the government subsidies or trade protection that are given to owners of industrial-sized factory farms.

SO, WHAT'S IN IT FOR YOU?

Well, for one thing, food that is eaten in season, fresh from the field, tastes great! There is no denying that a carrot grown in California, stored in a cold facility for some number of months and then shipped across the country cannot but fail in a taste test with a carrot grown down the road (or in your back yard), sweetened by the first frost of the season, harvested in the morning, scrubbed and on your plate by suppertime. The first will taste like a carrot, true, but the second will taste like a *Carrot*—sweet, juicy, vibrant and full of flavor.

Which is great. We all love to eat foods that taste better, but when you are trying to adhere to a budget, it is sometimes hard to justify paying twice as much for a carrot. But did you know that in addition to tasting like carrot heaven, that locally grown orange root is also packed with many times more nutrition? The average distance that food travels from farm to plate is variously placed somewhere between 1,500 to 3,000 miles, depending on where you live. In the week-long, or longer, delay from the field to your kitchen, sugars turn to starches (which is why that locally grown carrot tastes like candy and the one from miles away does not), plant cells shrink, and the produce loses nutrients. Folic acid, for instance, is thought to be very important in controlling heart disease. It is found in abundance in broccoli, but if the broccoli sits for longer than three days after harvest, the folic acid level is greatly depleted. When you eat broccoli fresh from the garden, however, you not only enjoy immense flavor, but increased health benefits as well.

In addition, when food is grown many miles away it is not allowed to ripen fully, as fully ripened fruits and vegetables are more prone to bruising in transit. When food is not allowed to reach its peak ripeness, its levels of powerful disease fighting nutrients and phytonutrients remain undeveloped. Not only does such unripened produce lack in flavor, it is also less able to keep us healthy.

In fact, the nutrient content of conventionally grown fruits and vegetables has plummeted over the last 50 years. When researchers looked at USDA data collected from 1950 through 1999 on nutrients in 43 crops, they found that, on average, the levels of all three evaluated minerals had declined, the levels of two of the five evaluated vitamins had declined, and the protein content had dropped by 6 percent. Researchers believe the declines may be caused by decades of hybridizing food crops for high yield. In other words, the older heirloom varieties of fruits and vegetables, the ones favored by many small local farms, not only have more flavor, they are also higher in nutrition.

Heirloom varieties might also be the fruits and vegetables that contain the genes that will thrive in a climate changing due to global warming, or that will prove capable of surviving pest and disease outbreaks. Large scale farmers stay away from these varieties, though, because they don't tolerate long-distance shipping, they yield smaller harvests, and they don't look as pretty as the hybrids of today's market.

But it is not just fruits and vegetables that need protecting from a loss of diversity. Small farmers today are working hard to preserve lines of heritage pigs, turkeys, cows and chickens. Cornish Cross chickens, Broad-Breasted White turkeys, and Holstein cows have replaced older non-hybrid breeds that may not grow as large as fast, lay as many eggs or produce as much milk, but they produce milk, eggs and meat that are far healthier for us.

Michael Pollan points out that when there is diversity in the diet, there is, of necessity, diversity in the fields and orchards. If there is more diversity in the fields, fewer chemical fertilizers and pesticides are required to sustain their growth. When we use fewer chemicals, we have healthier soil, water and air. Which means, of course, healthier plants and, therefore, healthier humans. It is all connected!

Eating seasonal foods also encourages more variety in the diet and consumption of different plant parts. In the spring, the vegetables we eat are primarily young leaves, such as lettuce and spinach; shoots, like asparagus (the part of the asparagus plant we eat is really a shoot that, if not cut down, will open up into a large ferny sort of arrangement); and unopened flowers, like broccoli and artichokes. In the summer, we feast on the fruits of flowers we have not consumed: berries, tomatoes, peppers and melons. Late summer and fall find us harvesting more fully ripened fruits, like winter squash. In the winter, roots such as carrots, parsnips, turnips and rutabagas become a mainstay of the menu. Over the course of a year, we end up eating a varied diet, from a wide range of the plant kingdom, which nourishes us with a full complement of vitamins, minerals and other nutrients.

Most of us are familiar with the components of nutrition that are often featured by the media: the dangers of saturated fats, the need to reduce our intake of red meat, the benefits of assorted vitamins, and so forth. We have come to associate various foods with certain nutrients — oranges with vitamin C, for instance, or carrots with vitamin A. What many people are not as aware of, however, is the variety of foods that contain those nutrients that are essential for keeping our bodies running at optimum levels. There is a great deal of vitamin C, for instance, in potatoes and cabbages, so it is still quite possible to incorporate a plentiful amount of that nutrient in your diet even if you do not have freshly-squeezed orange juice every day of the year.

Eating foods that are grown locally and in season also discourages eating endless meals of processed foods that are loaded with preservatives, high fructose corn syrup and salt. There has been much publicity recently about the increase in obesity in both children and adults, and the corresponding rise in childhood diabetes. In fact, what was once termed "adult-onset" diabetes has now been renamed Type II diabetes, due to the fact that the number of children being diagnosed with the disease has increased so drastically. As a nation, we are plagued by an increase in food related illnesses brought on, in large part, by the vast accessibility of inexpensive processed food. Were we to reduce our dependence on processed food, it would do much to curb obesity, obesity-related diabetes, heart disease, hypertension, and a host of other diet-related woes.

A diet based on foods that are grown elsewhere and transported can, in fact, be downright hazardous to your health. Products enduring long-distance transport and long-term storage often depend on preservatives and additives such as salt and sugar to make the journey. They also encounter numerous opportunities for contamination.

The past few years have seen a marked increase in outbreaks of infections such as e. coli and salmonella from both produce and meats. In the case of bacteria associated with produce, such as spinach, it is often unclear if the contamination originated at the restaurant or the farms or some point in between. What is clear, according to the *New York Times*, is that "illnesses have risen sharply because people are eating more fresh produce and wanting it year-round, leading to an increase in imports from countries with less stringent sanitary standards." As Joan Dye Gussow points out, where is the logic in eating a raspberry grown in a country where you wouldn't drink the water?

When you choose food that has been raised in your community, however, you have the opportunity to see for yourself how the animals are treated, how the vegetables are raised, and how the land is cared for. In addition, food that is raised on small local farms does not need repeated applications of chemical fertilizers and pesticides. Farmers who raise food on a smaller scale, employing centuries-old methods of intercropping and succession planting, do not deplete the soil, and their crops are not as vulnerable to the pests found in vast mono-cropped fields. Not only are those pesticides, herbicides and chemical fertilizers products of the petroleum industry, and thus subject to rising oil costs and depleted oil supplies, they are also harmful to the earth and its inhabitants. It has been demonstrated repeatedly that herbicide and pesticide residues do not wash off the skins of our apples and grapes. These residues are ingested by our children, whose developing systems are much more vulnerable to the effects of toxins. It has been suggested that many food allergies might be reactions to pesticides, as opposed to a reaction to specific food allergens.

When pesticides and herbicides are used in the fields, the runoff finds its way into our water supply, affecting aquatic and other wild life, as well as our drinking water. Recent studies show that the water supply of every major city in our country has measurable levels of agricultural and manufacturing chemicals—and these chemicals remain in the water even after it has been treated.

And we need to eat close to home for our kids! Many children these days grow up without vegetable gardens. They don't learn that peas and strawberries are ready to munch in June, that peaches are ripe in August, and that sweet creamy butternut squash is ready to come off the vine when it is time to go back to school. We need to teach our children the rhythm of the seasons to help them stay connected to the earth, and learn that it is the *earth* that provides us with food, not the grocery store.

FEED A FARMER, SAVE A TOWN

Eating food grown close to home is good for your community. When you purchase produce grown by a local farmer, the money you pay is recirculated within your community. Studies show that the share of the consumer's food dollar that is retained by the farming community dropped from more than forty cents in 1910 to just above seven cents in 1997. The typical U.S. wheat farmer, for example, now gets just six cents of each dollar spent on a loaf of bread. Think of how many items end up in your grocery cart each week for which you pay more for the packaging and marketing than for the contents you eat!

Moreover, when you buy food that has been grown on a huge industrial farm, you put your money into the hands of one of the multinational corporations that control today's food sources. When you patronize your local farmer, however, you support a member of a vanishing breed. Fewer than one million Americans now claim farming as their primary occupation. In Oregon, the average age of the farmer is 55, and only 5% are under the age of 35. But it is our local farmers who are imbued with the knowledge of which plants and animals thrive in our watershed. What will we do when the last farmer in our community finally throws up her or his hands, and the knowledge of how to grow food on that particular piece of land, with its unique soil structure and microclimate, is lost?

The loss of small local farms has more than a monetary effect on the community. It affects the spirit of the community as well. As industrial agriculture replaces family farms, there are fewer and less meaningful jobs and less local spending. Profits go to absentee landlords and distant suppliers, resulting in a net drain on the local community. Brian Halweil, in his book, *Eat Here*, describes a study conducted over half a century ago of two small towns in the San Joaquin Valley of California. The towns were alike in basic economic and geographic dimensions, including the value of agricultural production, but differed in farm sizes. It was found that there was an inverse correlation between the size of the farms and the well-being of the communities of which they were part. The small-farm community supported about 20% more people, at a higher level of living. There were lower poverty rates, lower levels of economic and social class distinctions, and lower crime rates. The majority of the small-farm community residents were independent entrepreneurs. In the large-farm town, only 20% of the residents owned their own businesses, with most other residents working as agricultural laborers. In the town with more small local farms, there were more business establishments, parks, schools, newspapers, civic organizations, churches, and a better physical infrastructure. Why? Folks living in that community had a financial and emotional investment in it. Money stayed in the community and was used to support and enhance the lives of those who lived there.

There is also evidence that, contrary to what many people believe, small farms are actually more productive than large ones, producing as much as 1,000 percent more output per unit of area. Recent studies show that a four-acre farm averages a net profit of $1,400 per acre. In comparison, a 1,364-acre farm yields $39 per acre. Why is this? Big farm advantages are always calculated on the basis of how much of a *single* crop the land will yield per acre. The greater productivity of a smaller more complex farm is calculated on the basis of how much food *overall* is produced per acre. The smaller farm can grow crops of varying root depths, plant heights, and nutrients simultaneously. Eating food grown in your community supports the people who have, through their hard work, acquired the knowledge of how to coax a whole lot of food out of one piece of earth.

Supporting your local farmer also helps preserve open space, protecting rich fertile soil from the advance of strip malls and housing developments, and protecting our air and soil from the pollution that accompanies such development. Protecting farms keeps your taxes from increasing. Unlike suburban developments, farms contribute more in taxes than they require in local services. On average, for every one dollar in revenue raised by residential development, the government must spend $1.17 on services, thus requiring higher taxes of all taxpayers. In comparison, for each dollar of revenue raised by farms, forests and open spaces, the government spends 34 cents on services.

SAVING THE WORLD, ONE STRAWBERRY AT A TIME

When we eat strawberries grown in New Zealand in the middle of December, it does not just affect our own health and that of our community. It affects the entire planet. The rise in international food trade and the proliferation of heavily processed and packaged foods has had enormous impacts on our environment. We humans devote a tremendous share of the Earth's surface to food production. The way our food is now produced greatly affects our rivers, wetlands, forests, oceans and atmosphere. It has been said that food production rivals transportation as the human activity with the greatest impact on the environment. A meat-rich meal made with imported ingredients, for instance, has a carbon footprint nine times greater than a vegetarian meal made with domestically produced ingredients. Today, the typical American meal contains ingredients from at least five countries outside the U.S!

Until the 1950s, almost all the fruits and vegetables consumed by Americans were grown on local farms. But the development of refrigerated long-haul trucks, the availability of inexpensive gasoline, and the development of the interstate highway system changed all that. By the end of the twentieth century, Americans had become accustomed to eating Florida oranges in the middle of winter, even in upstate New York. Of course the trend toward eating food grown elsewhere on the planet is not limited to the United States. Cows raised in England end up in restaurants in Japan, having been transported first by large refrigerated container trains to England's west coast, then loaded on a ship bound for the far east, before finally being trucked to the consumer in Japan. Today, some 898 million *tons* of food are shipped around the planet each year. And all this shipping consumes vast quantities of resources. A head of lettuce grown in Salinas Valley, California, for instance, and shipped to Washington, D.C., requires 36 times the fossil fuel energy for transport as it provides in food energy.

When you purchase locally grown foods you are taking one more step to lessen your footprint, doing one more thing to reduce global warming. Every time you cook a meal using food grown nearby, you are reducing the need for food grown on a distant field that must be transported, refrigerated and processed. Moreover, because transportation is just one piece of the global warming puzzle, every time you choose a whole food, as opposed to a processed one, you are taking yet another step. In calculating the carbon footprint of any food, the entire cycle needs to be examined: from the way the seeds are planted, by diesel tractor or by hand; how the crops are raised, with chemical fertilizers and herbicides, or not, in a heated hothouse or an open field; the method of harvest and storage, direct from farm to consumer or stored in a controlled temperature facility; to the amount of processing the food undergoes before it reaches your table.

IT'S ORGANIC BUT...

Industrial agriculture is not limited to conventionally grown produce. Wal-Mart has now joined many other large chain stores in including organic produce in their selection of fresh, frozen and processed foods. On the one hand, this is very exciting. Wasn't having organic food available to and desired by the masses part of the original dream of the organic movement? On the other hand, in order to meet the huge demand created by the superstores, "organic" has become an industry. To be sure, the fields are not being doused with pesticides and herbicides, and the fertilizers are not derived from petro-chemicals. None the less, on these industrial-sized organic farms, crops are grown in vast swaths of monoculture, and are packaged and shipped long distances, as is conventionally grown produce. To meet Wal-Mart's commitment to sell organic food at a mere ten percent above the cost of conventional products, food is sourced from wherever it can be grown most cheaply — and too often, that means in a country other than the U.S. We now have products that many people refer to as industrial organic — potatoes that might not have their peels laden with pesticides and fungicides, but which are still grown at the expense of a healthy ecosystem and in a manner dependant on fossil fuels.

WHAT, NO BANANAS?!

We have become a nation unable to feed itself. We urgently need to establish a more sustainable, secure food system. It is likely that the changing climate and rising oil prices will increasingly disrupt the intercontinental web of food production, making dependence on food from overseas, or across the country, more expensive and less dependable. As abrupt changes in the price of fuel affect the cost of running tractors, making fertilizer and pumping water, farmers who learn to raise crops with methods that are less dependent on petroleum products will be better off, as will the communities who have cultivated local food sources.

Do we have to give up *all* imported food? Probably not. Coffee, tea, spices and cocoa beans, for instance, can all be shipped without refrigeration, and are low in water content, which means they are lighter, and therefore require less fuel to get from one place to another. As long as we can grow and transport these foods in a fair and earth-friendly fashion, it will probably make sense to continue to trade them. Even foods that are higher in water content may continue to be shipped across country, but in greatly decreased quantities. Instead of expecting a glass of freshly-squeezed orange juice every day, we may need to view that juice as a luxury item, to be enjoyed less frequently — and with more appreciation.

Most importantly, we need to let the rhythm of our eating follow the dance of the seasons, and not allow ourselves to fall prey to Perpetual Summer Syndrome, wherein the succulent fruits of summer appear week after week in the aisles of the produce section, tempting us to believe that they are the real actors, not look-alike stand-ins. The Endless Summer is not a movie you want playing at your dinner table. Instead of feeling deprived when we walk past those red (tasteless) strawberries in February, we can anticipate what an explosion of flavor there will be in June when we pop one in our mouth, still warm from the sun. And in the meantime, enjoy a cobbler made from last summer's frozen berries!

CAN WE DO IT?

This question—can we feed ourselves with local foods—is being pondered by an increasing number of people. Some years ago, Joan Dye Gussow, author of *Confessions of a Suburban Gardener*, proved that she could feed herself year round largely from food grown in her upstate New York garden, or produced by farms that could easily be visited in one day.

In 2005, Alisa Smith and J.B. MacKinnon took on a project called The Hundred Mile Diet. They vowed to live for one year buying only food and drink that was produced within 100 miles of their home in Vancouver, B.C. To avoid being social outcasts, they allowed themselves to eat occasionally in restaurants or at friends' houses. And if they happened to be traveling, they allowed themselves to bring home foods grown within a hundred miles of that new locale. It was difficult, particularly at first, to locate sources of such basics as grains (which had at one time been grown on nearby farms) and protein (it was difficult, for instance, to find locally grown soybeans and a producer of tofu in their corner of British Columbia). However, not only did they survive, but they motivated a great many other people to attempt similar undertakings. They have developed an inspiring website, **100milediet.org**, which includes a page that helps you determine the 100 mile radius around your own home, and have published a book describing their year of eating locally grown foods, aptly named *Plenty*. Barbara Kingsolver has also written a book detailing her family's year of eating local foods in Virginia (*Animal, Vegetable, Miracle*), as has Gary Paul Nabhan (*Coming Home to Eat*). There is even a name for those who choose to eat food grown primarily in their surrounding watershed: locavore.

Closer to my home, the University of Portland cafeteria, along with 190 other corporate and college cafeterias, participated in an "Eat Local Challenge," organized by Bon Appétit Management Company. They asked chefs to feature a lunch option made entirely from ingredients obtained within a 150 mile radius of their respective kitchens. Portland's staff took it a step further and included every item on the lunch menu. They banned virtually all oils, sugar, spices, citrus, mayonnaise and mustard. Processed meats were replaced with locally raised beef and chicken. Bread was baked with grain grown in Reardan, Washington. They even made their own salt—25 gallons of seawater were boiled down to 5½ pounds of crystals. Even the Pepsi machine was decommissioned. Students learned about the challenge from cards placed on cafeteria tables. They reported that in addition to supporting the effort because of their commitment to eating local foods, they were in favor of it because of the delicious food: latkes made with smoked salmon and dill and drizzled with crème fraîche, and gnocchi served with a Tillamook white cheddar sauce and green beans, for instance. Who wouldn't be happy to have their Swiss steak replaced with a menu like that?

In fact, the Willamette Valley has recently seen a surge of people and organizations interested in relocalizing their food sources. Portland and Eugene both host chapters of Slow Food, groups who come together to celebrate the relaxed creation of home-cooked meals. Portland also boasts a wonderful magazine and website called Edible Portland (see "Eat Local" in Helpful Websites). There are a burgeoning number of local food networks in Eugene, among them the Willamette Valley Food Coalition, which hosts regular community potluck dinners at which everyone brings a dish composed of locally grown food. In the Corvallis area, a non-profit organization called the Ten Rivers Food Web (named after the ten major rivers that define the area's watershed) is working to collaborate with other organizations to plan events that heighten awareness and create connections between food producers and communities.

It is possible to feed ourselves with locally grown foods, and to feed ourselves well! Here in the Pacific Northwest, we are blessed with a relatively benign climate, as well as abundant natural resources. Whether you qualify "local" as being within a 100 mile radius of your home, or the distance that can be reached in one day by car, train, bicycle or on boot, the bottom line seems to be that we need to focus on re-learning how to cook according to the seasons, support local growers so that they can supply us with produce, grain and meat, and find ways to import from as close at hand as possible what we cannot grow here in a sustainable manner.

HERE ARE SOME WAYS TO GET STARTED

1. Learn the seasons in your area. When does spring begin — not just according to the calendar, but according to your particular microclimate?

2. Learn the foods available in your area during each season. For instance, fresh local melons may be available in June in California, but in the Pacific Northwest, they are not ripe until August.

3. Learn to cook with seasonal foods and how to substitute ingredients in recipes. If the recipe you choose for dinner in January calls for fresh basil, pull out a cube of puréed basil and olive oil from the freezer and use that instead.

4. Resist the urge to buy out-of-season produce. Keep in mind what a celebration that asparagus will be when you eat it fresh from your garden or local farm.

5. Buy large quantities of food while it is in season and freeze, dry or can it. Or find someone in your community who puts food up and buy from them.

6. Ask your grocery store where its produce is grown. If they don't know, ask them to find out and to post that information.

7. If you do buy food grown abroad or from the other side of the country, focus on foods that are low in water content. Fresh fruit and vegetables require more fossil fuels to ship and cool than coffee, tea, cocoa beans and spices which are lighter and don't require refrigeration.

8. When you can't find locally grown and/or locally processed food, choose food products that contain a minimal number of ingredients and that require a minimum of processing. For instance, instead of purchasing polenta in a tube, buy coarsely ground corn meal (polenta) and make your own.

9. Grow your own food. If you can't grow it, buy food that was grown within a leisurely day's drive from your home.

10. Investigate alternative methods of growing. A simple cold frame or hoop structure can easily extend the harvest season to include all twelve months of the year.

11. Develop a purchasing ladder to streamline your decision making process when you shop. When true local is not available, determine the next most sustainable alternative. If you do the research ahead of time, it is easier to adhere to when you are pushing a grocery cart down the aisle with a tired hungry child.

12. Shop the edges of the grocery store. Mass-produced foods are the least likely to be locally sourced and are generally shelved in the center of the store. Vegetables, fruit, dairy and bulk goods are typically found around the store's perimeter.

THE SEASONS, WHAT IS AVAILABLE, AND WHAT TO DO WITH IT

It's difficult
to think anything
but pleasant thoughts
while eating
a home-grown tomato.

—Lewis Grizzard

Following is a chart of the typical availability of common fruits and vegetables in the Pacific Northwest. Keep in mind that in any given year, there will be some variability in harvest times due to the vagaries of weather. Then, too, the Pacific Northwest contains a wide range of microclimates, so some fruits and vegetables may be available at an earlier or later time than indicated here. Finally, some produce, such as carrots and onions, will often be available year-round as the harvest season merges with cold storage, and the harvest period of other vegetables can be extended by the use of row covers and hoop houses.

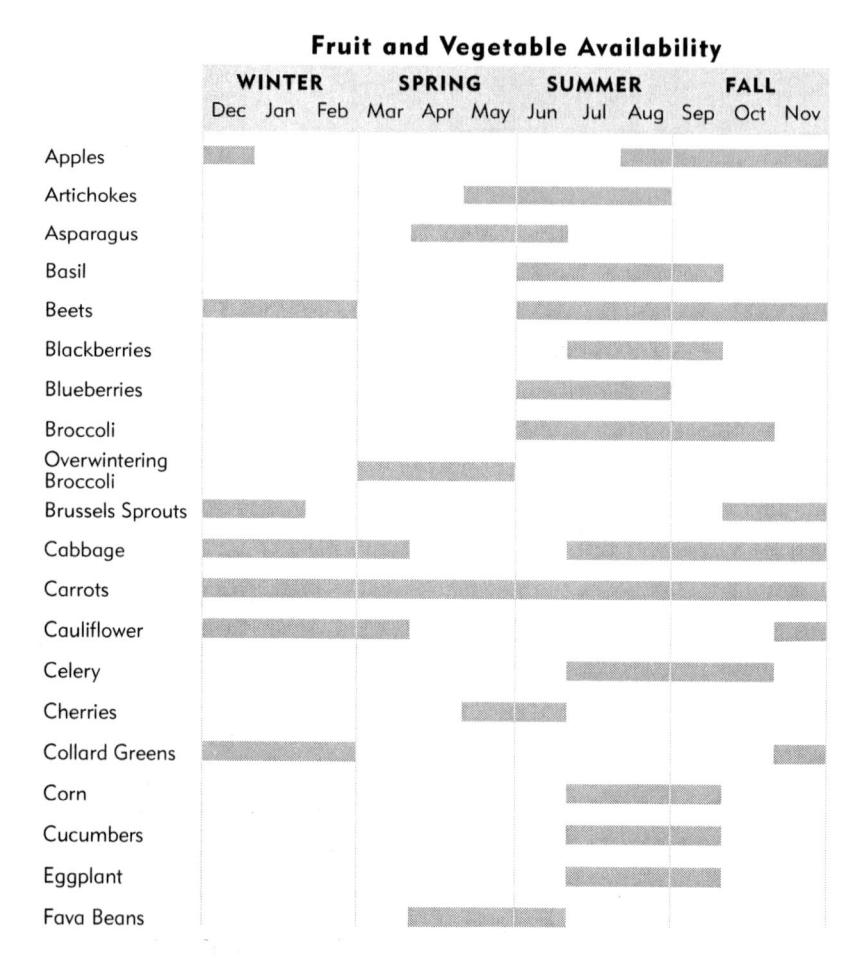

Fruit and Vegetable Availability

Produce	Availability
Apples	Dec–Jan; Aug–Nov
Artichokes	May–Jul
Asparagus	Apr–May
Basil	Jul–Sep
Beets	Dec–Feb; Jul–Nov
Blackberries	Jul–Sep
Blueberries	Jul–Sep
Broccoli	Jul–Oct
Overwintering Broccoli	Apr–May
Brussels Sprouts	Dec–Jan; Oct–Nov
Cabbage	Dec–Apr; Jul–Nov
Carrots	Dec–Nov (year-round)
Cauliflower	Dec–Apr; Nov
Celery	Jul–Oct
Cherries	Jun–Jul
Collard Greens	Dec–Feb; Oct–Nov
Corn	Jul–Sep
Cucumbers	Jul–Sep
Eggplant	Jul–Sep
Fava Beans	May–Jun

	WINTER	SPRING	SUMMER	FALL
	Dec Jan Feb	Mar Apr May	Jun Jul Aug	Sep Oct Nov
Garlic	██████████	██████████	██████████	██████████
Grapes			████████	██████
Green Beans			██████	████
Jerusalem Artichokes			██████	██████
Kale	██████	██████		████
Kohlrabi	██		████	██████
Leeks	████	████		████
Melons			████	
Mushrooms	██	██████	██████	██████
Mustard Greens	██	████		██████
Onions	██████	██████	██████	██████
Parsley	██	██████	██████	██████
Parsnips	██████	██		
Peas		████	████	██
Peaches			████	
Pears			██████	████
Peppers			████	████
Plums			████	██
Potatoes	██		████	██████
Radishes		██████		████
Raspberries			████	
Rhubarb		████	██	
Rutabagas	██████			██
Salad Greens		██████	████	
Spinach		██████		████
Strawberries			████	
Summer Squash			████	
Swiss Chard	██	██████	██████	██████
Tomatoes			████	████
Turnips	████		████	██████
Wild Greens	██	████		████
Winter Squash	██████	██		████

WINTER · December · January · February

December, the first real month of winter in the Pacific Northwest, is exciting. The holidays inspire festive feasts for feeding gatherings of friends and family. Great pots of stews and soups are as comforting to eat as they are fun to make. Even the weather is thrilling; the threat of snow on the valley floor is eagerly sought by children of all ages, even if the merest hint of the white stuff does bring traffic to a near stand still. Farmers and gardeners breathe a sigh of relief; the harvest is in and the rains and snows return to fill the rivers and aquifers.

By late January and early February, however, the raw cold rains become wearisome. Weather reports are scanned for hints, not of low snow levels, but of those few days or weeks when the Chinook winds blow through, bringing the promise of spring. Spring peepers strike up their evening chorus when the temperatures have moderated. One morning in February we wake to find the robins have brought their songs back to fill the sky. Seed racks return to the garden stores, teasing us into thoughts of sweet fresh peas, juicy tomatoes and ambrosial strawberries.

Late winter and early spring are perhaps the most challenging months, in many people's minds, to keep a diet based on local foods. Perhaps, though, we simply need to become familiar with what to do with the many root vegetables and brassicas that store well over the winter, and to become adept at incorporating frozen or preserved foods into our diet. Which does not mean we should eat boiled cabbage and soggy canned green beans all winter! It means acquiring a taste for, and a repertoire of recipes to utilize, such "forgotten" foods as parsnips, rutabagas, turnips, Jerusalem artichokes, leeks, kale and collard greens. It means, also, becoming accustomed to eating dried and frozen fruits, instead of "fresh" fruit shipped in from miles away. And it can mean combining foods in new ways to tempt the palate.

IN SEASON

The following produce can be considered "in season" during winter and early spring, even though it is not actually growing, just being stored in refrigerated units, root cellars, hall closets or simply in the ground:

Apples	**Jerusalem Artichokes**
Bean Sprouts	**Kale**
Beets	**Kohlrabi**
Burdock Root	**Onions**
Cabbage	**Parsnips**
Carrots	**Pears**
Celeriac	**Potatoes**
Collard Greens	**Rutabagas**
Cranberries	**Shallots**
Daikon Radish	**Turnips**
Garlic	**Winter Greens**
Hazelnuts	**Winter Squash and Pumpkins**

SEASON FEATURES

Carrots: Oh, sure, we all know the ubiquitous carrot. But have you had one fresh from the garden after the first frost? It will not even closely resemble your average supermarket carrot! Carrots are available nearly year-round now, but they really come into their own in the winter months. Carrot sticks are handy conveyance devices for any number of dips. Grated raw carrot can be mixed into green salad or a coleslaw, or stand on its own with a dressing of yogurt, a hint of fresh mint, nutmeg, and a squeeze of lemon juice. Or for an Asian sort of taste, mix some grated carrot with a bit of toasted sesame oil, grated fresh ginger, a splash of rice vinegar, and a bit of sugar. Carrots can also be roasted, braised, boiled and puréed.

Cauliflower is another vegetable that people tend not to get excited about but which really deserves more appreciation. They are a good winter crop here in the Pacific Northwest and can be used many ways. The florets can be eaten raw, or steamed and marinated for quick pickles. Cauliflower is good in curries, as it absorbs flavors very well. Chopped into one-inch pieces, cauliflower can be sautéed with garlic and tossed with pasta. Or just steam it and toss with caraway seed, dill, and a bit of yogurt or sour cream.

Celeriac: Also called celery root, celeriac is an odd-looking round root about the size of a large potato. It is a type of celery grown for its large top root which can be eaten raw or cooked after the tough outer surface has been peeled away. Celeriac is good cooked in soup or stew, or mashed alone or in combination with potatoes.

Collard Greens and Kale: These are related closely enough to be discussed together. As with many winter vegetables, they are best when the frost has nipped them, as it brings out their sweetness. Cut the tough stem from the middle by folding the leaf in half and trimming out the stem, then cut the leaf into ribbons or chunks. Add to soups and stews; sauté with garlic and olive oil; sauté with oil, garlic, minced ginger and a splash of soy sauce. You can also add the sautéed or steamed greens to mashed potatoes, pasta or rice.

Jerusalem Artichokes: Neither an artichoke nor from Jerusalem, these bumpy tubers are actually the root of a perennial flower that looks like a sunflower. The tubers, also called sunchokes, have a potato-like texture that is slightly sweet and a bit nutty, rather like a jicama or water chestnut. You can scrub them and eat them raw (although some people may find that raw sunchokes have a tendency to make them "windy"), or bake, boil, steam, fry or make a soup out of them—in short, treat them as you would a potato. They marry well with cinnamon and nutmeg, onions and cream, and can be substituted for turnips or parsnips—or added to a gratin containing these and other root vegetables.

Kohlrabi: A member of the cabbage family, kohlrabi looks like a turnip that has decided to grow above ground. When not allowed to grow to alarming proportions, kohlrabi has a nutty-sweet flavor and an apple-like texture. It can be peeled and grated and added to salads and slaws, or mixed with grated carrots, apples and beets, and dressed with a vinaigrette or creamy dressing. You can also slice it thinly as crudités for dips, or steam the slices and top with butter and chives or dill.

Parsnips: Have you tried a parsnip? They look like gnarly white carrots. Although not as tasty raw as carrots, when cooked parsnips are sweet and earthy at the same time—wonderful in soups and stews. They are best when harvested after a frost, which means that parsnips from California, besides lacking nutrition and flavor after having traveled so far, will be doubly insipid for not having sweetened up with a good cold blast of winter. My father's favorite way to cook parsnips is to peel them and cut them into matchsticks, then sauté them in a bit of butter until they are tender and starting to caramelize. Add a splash of brandy and a spoonful of brown sugar and cook a few more minutes. Traditional Christmas fare for us! Parsnips are also good boiled and mashed with potatoes—especially if you add a pinch or two of grated nutmeg.

Rutabagas are very often confused with turnips, especially at the checkout stand of the grocery store. They are, in fact, shaped rather like a turnip, with one end of the bulbous root being purplish, but the other end is a creamy yellow, rather than white like a turnip. The flesh, too, is cream colored. Like turnips and kohlrabi, they are good when grated or julienned raw and tossed with other root vegetables in a winter slaw, when tossed in olive oil with other vegetables and roasted, and when steamed and mashed alone or in combination with other vegetables such as potatoes or parsnips. Rutabagas are also sometimes known as Swedes, and are a very common winter vegetable in Sweden.

Turnips are roots that are very mild and tender when harvested young in the spring. After a fall harvest turnips will hold in your root cellar most of the winter. Grate young raw turnips into salads, or make a slaw of grated turnip, apple and carrot, with a dressing of lemon juice, olive oil, chives and dill. Turnips can be added to soups and stews, or mashed with potatoes. Or make a simple turnip bake by steaming slices of turnips and then layering them in a baking dish with sliced apples and cheddar cheese. Bake until the apples are tender and the cheese is melted.

Winter Greens: I am referring here to the many types of salad greens that can be planted in the fall and harvested all winter if covered by a hoop house or cold frame. The list includes arugula, Italian dandelion, parsley, claytonia (also known as miner's lettuce which many consider to be a weed), mâche, radicchio, sorrel, spinach and sugarloaf chicory. Some of these may be found in supermarkets; many can be found in farmers markets (although often farmers markets are closed during the mid-winter months). If you are a member of a CSA your farmer may provide you with winter greens. Or grow your own! Either way, a salad from some of these wilder greens tossed with a light dressing of olive oil and lemon juice can chase away the winter blues like nothing else.

Winter Squash: Winter squash are good for much more than table decorations, although they grow in such a bountiful array of sizes, shapes and colors that they do lend themselves to creating visual, as well as edible, feasts. Larger squash, like butternut, can be peeled and cut into chunks and steamed and then mashed. Or you can cut a squash in half, scoop out the seeds, and bake it cut side down at 350°F, until a fork can easily pierce the skin and the inside is very tender—about 30 to 50 minutes, depending on the size. Scoop out the flesh and purée. Baking the squash takes a bit longer, but concentrates the sugars more. This is more practical with a butternut than a huge kabocha, but even the mammoth guys can be cut into chunks and baked.

Smaller thin-skinned squash like delicata or acorn can be cut in half and baked, cut side down on a lightly greased pan at 350–375°F for 30 to 50 minutes, until tender. Once the halves are baked, they can be flipped over, drizzled with butter and sprinkled with brown sugar and cinnamon (my kids' favorite). Alternatively, you can stuff the squash with any number of fillings and reheat them before serving. Or try roasting your squash and your garlic at the same time: Halve and scoop out a winter squash, then fill the seed cavity with 4 or 5 *unpeeled* garlic cloves and a few fresh sage leaves. Drizzle with olive oil and sprinkle with salt and pepper. Roast at 400°F until tender—about 30 minutes. Let cool until you are able to handle them, then peel the garlic cloves or squeeze the garlic out, remove the sage leaves, and mash the garlic into the squash with a fork.

If you are awash in squash, consider baking a quantity of them, scooping out their innards, puréeing and then freezing the purée in small batches. The roasted purée is great for thickening soups and stews, or adding to baked goods. Try mixing it with mashed potatoes, or using "squished squash" as a topping for shepherd's pie instead of mashed potatoes.

WHITE BEAN DIP

1½ cups dry cannellini or other white beans soaked and cooked, or one 15-ounce can

3 Tablespoons olive oil

plus either

¼ cup chopped fresh parsley

2 Tablespoons grated Parmesan cheese

2 teaspoons minced fresh or 1 teaspoon dried oregano

1 large clove garlic, minced finely or put through garlic press

or

2 Tablespoons lemon juice

1 large clove garlic, minced finely or put through garlic press

¾ teaspoon ground cumin

1 Tablespoon chopped fresh mint or 1 teaspoon dried

1 Tablespoon dill (frozen or dried)

1 teaspoon grated lemon peel

Combine all ingredients in a food processor and process until smooth. Season with salt and pepper to taste, and drizzle a bit more olive oil over the surface if you like. Serve with crackers, bread and/or raw vegetables.

PESTO LOG

Adapted from *Still Life with Menu*, Mollie Katzen.

½ cup pesto (see Putting Food By)

8 ounces cream cheese

1 cup ricotta cheese

Garnishes: sprigs of sage, thyme, parsley

Mix the cream cheese and ricotta cheese in a small bowl until it is smooth and easy to work with. Spread a two-layer rectangle of cheesecloth, approximately 6 x 18 inches in size, on a baking sheet. Spread the cheese mixture on the cheesecloth, leaving a 2-inch margin all the way around. Refrigerate uncovered for a few hours so that the cheese firms up.

Spread the pesto onto the cheese layer, leaving ½ inch clear all the way around. Lift the cheesecloth from one of the long sides and roll it up, as you would sushi, into a log shape. Wrap the log snugly in the cheesecloth and place it back on the baking sheet. Cover tightly with plastic wrap and refrigerate at least overnight so that the pesto melds with the cheeses.

The next day, unwrap the log and place it on a platter. Decorate it with your garnish of choice, and serve with crackers, bread and/or raw vegetables.

CLAUDIA'S MUSHROOM CROSTINI

Claudia was a member of the Monday Play Group, a loose affiliation of women who met weekly for many years while our children were young. She hailed from Italy, so play group at her house was always delicious.

Slice a baguette or loaf of crusty bread into ½-inch thick pieces. Brush with olive oil and put under the broiler until crisp. Rub the toasted bread with a garlic clove.

Chop fresh mushrooms in a food processor. Sauté the mushrooms with butter or olive oil. Mix with cream cheese. Top the crostini with a layer of the mushroom mix and some grated Parmesan. Broil until the cheese melts.

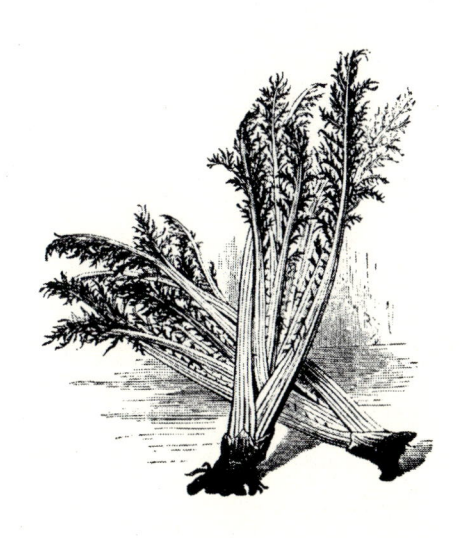

WINTER SALADS

Salads in the winter do not have to consist of lettuce that has been grown in California and shipped north. Shredded cabbage, grated carrot, kohlrabi, turnip and other root vegetables can be mixed with toasted chopped nuts, dried fruit, chopped apples or pears, and mixed with your favorite salad dressing.

KALE SALAD

Rinse a bunch of kale. Cut out the tough inner ribs, then slice the leaves into ribbons. Steam until the kale is slightly wilted, about 3 to 5 minutes. When cool, toss with a mix of 1½ tablespoons soy sauce, 1 tablespoon sesame oil, 1 clove garlic (pressed) and a 1-inch chunk of fresh ginger (grated). Serve at room temperature. When it is in season, you can do the same thing with chard.

UNBELIEVABLY GOOD COLESLAW

Adapted from *Sacramental Magic in a Small-Town Café*, Br. Peter Reinhart.

1 small head green cabbage or half a large head, grated or shredded

1 or 2 carrots, grated

½ small onion, finely diced
(Walla Wallas are very nice, if they are available)

DRESSING

¾ cup mayonnaise

⅛ cup cider vinegar

¼ cup sugar

½ teaspoon ground pepper

Combine the cabbage, carrots and onion in a bowl. Mix the dressing ingredients. Pour the dressing over the vegetables and toss well. Adjust the balance of mayonnaise, sugar and vinegar, until you achieve the perfect combination of sweet and sour, peppery and creamy. Let the slaw sit for an hour before serving. You can use red cabbage too, which will tint everything a rosy pink if it sits long enough.

CABBAGE AND APPLE SALAD

1 crispy apple, coarsely grated or chopped

½ small head green cabbage, shredded

½ cup or more roasted nut of your choice: walnuts, hazelnuts or almonds

DRESSING

¾ cup yogurt

Pinch each: nutmeg, cinnamon and allspice

2 to 3 teaspoons sugar

1 to 2 Tablespoons lemon juice

Toss the apple and cabbage together in a bowl. Whisk the dressing ingredients together and toss with the apple and cabbage. Add the nuts just before serving.

For a lighter alternative, leave out the yogurt, spices and nuts, and just toss the apple and cabbage with sugar and lemon juice, then, if you have them, mix in some chopped chives.

WINTERGREEN FARM CABBAGE SLAW

1 cabbage, thinly sliced

1 pound carrots, grated

1 bunch cilantro, chopped

⅓ cup lime juice

⅓ cup apple cider vinegar

2 Tablespoons salt

1 Tablespoon chili powder

Toss all ingredients. Let stand at room temperature for 1 hour before serving.

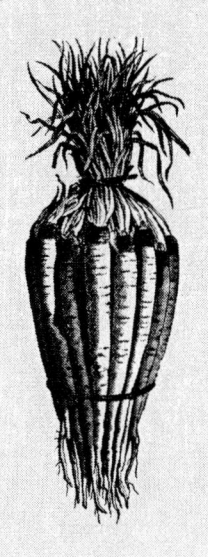

WINTER SOUPS

Save the bones! That was the refrain we inevitably heard at my mother's house as we cleaned up after a chicken or turkey dinner. Bones were hoarded in the freezer, and then hauled out from time to time to be dumped into a large soup pot, covered with water, and garnished with bits and ends of vegetables from the bin (sad looking pieces of onion, ends of celery, limp carrots, and so forth). A shot of vinegar (to pull the calcium from the bones, the better to nourish us), some peppercorns, a bay leaf, and whatever herbs were at hand, were tossed in. After a good 4-hour simmer, the mess was strained and a lovely broth resulted: the base of most every soup that issued from my mother's kitchen.

You can adopt the same practice with vegetables. Save the ends of celery, the peelings of onions, bits of squash, and boil them up with some carrots and herbs to make a vegetable broth. If you roast the vegetables first, the resulting stock will be very rich.

BEAN SOUP MIX

Anasazi beans, pinto beans, black turtle beans, black-eyed peas, Great Northern beans, baby lima beans, large lima beans, green and yellow split peas, small red beans, adzuki beans, barley. Go have fun in your local bulk foods section, filling bags with fairly equal amounts of each of the above. Take them home, mix in a big jar, and when you need a pot of soup, retrieve about 2 cups of the mix and off you go! This is my favorite blend of beans, but obviously, the variations are endless. Anasazi beans, however, are *really* good if you can get them — they are so creamy!

MIGHTY FINE BEAN SOUP

2 cups Bean Soup Mix (see page 50)

1 bay leaf

2 quarts water

2 smoked ham hocks

1 Tablespoon olive oil

1 large onion, chopped

1 large clove garlic, or more, minced

Salt and pepper to taste

1-quart jar of tomatoes, chopped, juice reserved, or 1 large can plum tomatoes, or an equivalent amount of frozen tomatoes

1½ teaspoons chili powder or 1 chopped chili pepper or ¼ teaspoon red pepper flakes

Juice of 1 large lemon

Rinse the beans and soak them overnight in cold water to cover. Or do a quick soak by bringing the beans to a boil, removing the pot from the heat and letting it sit for 1 hour. Drain. In a good-sized soup pot, brown the ham hocks and sauté the onions and garlic until softened. Add 2 quarts fresh water, the bay leaf and beans, and bring to a boil. Cover and simmer for 2 hours, until the beans are just tender. Add salt and pepper to taste, the tomatoes and their juices, the chili powder or pepper or pepper flakes, and the lemon juice. Remove the meat from the ham hocks. Chop the meat and return it to the pot. Simmer until the beans are very tender and the flavors have become well acquainted. As with many soups, this one is even better the next day.

CURRIED WINTER VEGETABLE SOUP

Adapted from the now-defunct *Kitchen Garden* magazine.

1 Tablespoon olive oil

1 Tablespoon curry powder, or more to taste

1 onion, chopped

4 cups vegetable or chicken stock

½ cup lentils (the small red ones are nice)

1 large potato, diced

1 turnip, diced

1 parsnip, diced

2 carrots, diced

¼ cup coconut milk

2 teaspoons chopped cilantro

Salt to taste

In a soup pot, heat the oil and add the onion and curry powder. Sauté until the onion is soft, but not browned. Add the stock and lentils, bring to a boil, then reduce to a simmer. Cook, covered, over medium heat, until the lentils are soft—about 10 minutes for the red kind, longer for brown lentils. Season with salt to taste.

Add the potato, turnip, parsnip and carrot. Simmer, covered, until the vegetables are soft but not mushy, about 25 minutes. Remove from heat. Add the coconut milk and cilantro. Season with salt.

MOM'S FAVORITE SALMON CHOWDER

You can often find a relatively inexpensive tail piece of salmon at the fish market—that works just fine. Dinner in under 45 minutes!

2 cups chicken broth

1 bottle clam juice (optional)

2 pounds fresh salmon

6 Tablespoons butter (or half olive oil)

1 onion, chopped

2 stalks celery, chopped

¼ teaspoon each: dry basil, thyme, and marjoram or oregano

¼ cup minced parsley

1½ cups milk

1 Tablespoon brandy

One 14-ounce can chopped tomatoes or 2 frozen tomatoes

Salt and pepper to taste

Grated sharp cheddar

Crisp bacon, crumbled (optional)

If you are using bacon, fry it in a skillet, then remove it to a paper towel to drain. In that skillet, combine the broth, clam juice (if using), and wine. Bring to a boil, then lower to a simmer. Poach the salmon in the broth until tender and opaque. Remove the salmon, cool, take off the skin and remove the bones. Break the salmon into pieces and set aside. In a soup pot, melt the butter/oil and sauté the onion and celery until soft. Stir in the basil, thyme and marjoram, the tomatoes with their juices, and the poaching liquid. Cover and simmer for 10 minutes. Add the salmon pieces, brandy, and salt and pepper to taste. Serve with bowls of parsley, grated cheese and bacon to sprinkle on top.

SALMON AND CORN CHOWDER

It is getting easier to find locally caught salmon and tuna from boats that use hook and line rather than drift nets. If you have fresh salmon, use it, but some good quality canned salmon from the pantry makes this an easy supper to put together.

6 Tablespoons butter or half olive oil

1 onion, chopped

2 stalks celery, chopped

2 carrots, diced

¾ teaspoon thyme

3 large cloves garlic, minced

3 potatoes, diced

1 to 2 cups frozen corn

2 cups water, chicken stock, fish stock, or a combination

2 cans salmon or 1 pound fresh salmon fillet, skin and bones removed

2½ to 3 cups milk — part of this can be cream, amount depending on your taste buds and arteries

½ cup white wine (optional)

Melt the butter/heat oil in a soup pot. Add the onion, celery, carrots, garlic and thyme and sauté until soft, about 3 minutes. Stir in the potatoes and broth/water/clam juice. Cover and cook, until the potatoes are tender. Add the corn, salmon and wine (if using). Cover and simmer gently until the corn and salmon are heated thoroughly (or, if using fresh fish, until the fish is nearly opaque) — about 10 minutes. (When using fresh fish, add the fillet in one piece and it will break apart as it cooks.) Add the milk and/or cream and cook until heated but not boiling. Season with salt and pepper to taste.

This is also good with fresh white fish, such as Pacific halibut, white sea bass or Pacific cod, all of which are fairly abundant, well managed and fished in an environmentally-responsible manner.

CARROT GINGER SOUP

2 pounds carrots

4 cups water

1 Tablespoon butter

1 large onion, chopped

2 cloves garlic, minced

2 Tablespoons fresh ginger, grated or minced

1½ teaspoons salt

¼ teaspoon ground fennel

¼ teaspoon cinnamon

¼ teaspoon ground allspice

1 cup coconut milk

Peel, trim and cut the carrots into 1-inch chunks. In a large pot, add the carrots to the water, cover and bring to a boil. Lower heat and simmer for 10 to 15 minutes, until soft. Meanwhile, in a frying pan, melt the butter and sauté the onions over low heat until they begin to soften, about 10 minutes. Add the garlic, ginger and spices and sauté another 10 minutes or so. Add the onion mixture, as well as the coconut milk, to the pot. Remove from heat. When it has cooled slightly, put the soup through a food mill or food processor until smooth. Gently reheat before serving.

CURRIED TOFU AND VEGETABLES

The spices are from my mother's "Oh No, Not Turkey Again!" a recipe she makes each year after Thanksgiving.

3 Tablespoons vegetable oil

2 to 3 teaspoons curry powder

Pinch cayenne

1 teaspoon tumeric

Dash each: nutmeg, cinnamon and ginger

2 Tablespoons whole coriander seeds

1 teaspoon cumin seeds

1 teaspoon mustard seeds

1 teaspoon cardamom seeds, removed from their shells

¼ teaspoon anise seeds

1 onion, chopped

3 cloves garlic, minced

2 cups cubed butternut squash

1 large potato, cubed

3 carrots, diced

1 cup cauliflower, broken onto small florets

¼ cup raisins

1 apple, diced

1 cup, or more, vegetable stock or water

1 block tofu, cubed

2 cups thinly sliced green cabbage, or substitute Brussels sprouts cut in half or quarters

Grind the coriander, cumin, mustard, cardamom and anise in a mortar and pestle or spice grinder. In a large skillet, heat the oil, add all the spices and heat until fragrant. Add the onion and sauté until soft. Add the garlic, squash, potato, carrots, raisins and apple and cook over low heat for 2 more minutes. Add the stock or water. Cover and cook until the vegetables begin to soften. Add the cabbage or Brussels sprouts, cauliflower and tofu. Cook until tender. Serve over rice. Garnish with peanuts or chutney.

JOANNA'S BEEF STEW

This needs to be started a day in advance, which makes it a good weekend dish.

2 pounds beef stew meat, cut into uniform chunks, about 1-inch square

1½ cups red wine

¼ cup brandy (optional)

2 Tablespoons olive oil

½ teaspoon thyme

½ teaspoon minced sage leaves

1 bay leaf

2 to 3 cloves garlic, mashed

1 onion, thinly sliced

2 carrots, thinly sliced

¼ cup chopped parsley

1½ cups fresh chopped mushrooms

2 cups whole tomatoes, roughly chopped (canned or frozen)

Marinate the beef chunks overnight in the wine, brandy (if using), olive oil, herbs, garlic, onion and carrots.

The next day, drain the beef, reserving the marinade and the vegetables. Preheat the oven to 325°F. Dredge the beef chunks in flour mixed with a bit of salt and pepper. Heat some olive oil in a skillet and brown the beef, working in batches so that the pieces are browned evenly. As each batch is browned, place a layer of beef in an oven-proof casserole dish or Dutch oven, and cover it with a layer of the marinated vegetables, the tomatoes, and then the mushrooms.

Pour the marinade over the meat and vegetables, adding stock if necessary, to almost cover. Simmer in the oven 3 to 4 hours. You can do this a day in advance, refrigerate it overnight and skim the fat from the top the next day before reheating.

BULGAR AND WINTER VEGETABLES

Adapted from a *Bon Appétit* magazine recipe.

2 Tablespoons olive oil

4 cups of ¾-inch pieces of chopped, peeled assorted root vegetables, such as carrots, turnips, parsnips, celeriac, etc.

1 large onion, chopped

3 cloves minced garlic, or more to taste

4 cups vegetable broth

¼ cup minced parsley

1 teaspoon oregano

1½ cups bulgar wheat

1 can garbanzo beans, drained and rinsed

1 package frozen spinach, thawed and drained, or 1 bunch fresh if available, or substitute winter greens

Salt and pepper to taste

Heat the oil in a large pot. Add the onions and garlic. Sauté until soft. Add the vegetables and sauté another 10 minutes. Add the broth, parsley and oregano. Bring to a boil. Add the bulgar wheat, cover and reduce heat to low. Simmer until the bulgar is almost tender, stirring occasionally, about 15 minutes. Add the spinach and garbanzo beans. Stir until heated. (If using winter greens, add them to the root vegetables toward the end of their sauté time.) Season with salt and pepper to taste. Some Parmesan or feta cheese sprinkled on top is nice.

STIFADO (GREEK BEEF STEW)

Another family recipe.

2 pounds lean stew beef

½ cup butter or olive oil

2 pounds small peeled fresh onions, or large onions, peeled and cut into chunks

1 bay leaf

6 ounces tomato paste

½ cup red wine

2 Tablespoons red wine vinegar

1 Tablespoon brown sugar

2 cloves garlic, mashed or minced

Pinch black pepper

¼ teaspoon salt

1 stick cinnamon

½ teaspoon whole cloves

¼ teaspoon ground cumin

¼ cup currants or raisins

¾ cup walnut halves

½ pound crumbled feta cheese or goat cheese

Put the stew meat in a Dutch oven with the butter or oil and heat until the butter is melted but the meat is not browned. Toss to coat. Add the onions and bay leaf. Mix in the tomato paste, wine, vinegar, sugar, garlic, salt, pepper, spices and raisins. Bring to a simmer and cook slowly for 3 hours, without stirring. Just before serving, toast the walnuts until lightly brown and crispy, then stir them and the cheese into the stew.

WINTER VEGETABLE GRATIN

Contributed by Lynne Fessenden, who adapted it from *Your Organic Kitchen*, by Jesse Ziff Cool. Feel free to play with the vegetable combinations. Unlike yams, sweet potatoes do grow in the Willamette Valley, but need a bit of coaching.

¼ **cup unbleached white flour**

¼ **cup brown sugar**

1 cup crumbled goat cheese and/or grated smoked Gouda

1 teaspoon salt

½ **teaspoon pepper**

1 small winter squash, such as butternut, peeled and thinly sliced (about ½ pound)

1 onion, peeled and thinly sliced

2 Yukon gold potatoes or other waxy potato, thinly sliced

1 fennel bulb, peeled and thinly sliced

2 rutabagas, peeled and thinly sliced

2 sweet potatoes, thinly sliced, if not available locally, add more potato or squash

2 cups milk

½ **cup grated Parmesan cheese, or substitute more smoked Gouda or goat cheese**

In a small bowl, combine the flour, sugar, salt and pepper. Mix in the goat cheese and set aside. In a greased 2-quart baking dish or gratin pan, layer one third of the vegetables—all sliced as thin as possible. Sprinkle with one third of the flour-cheese mixture. Continue layering vegetables and the flour-cheese mixture, finishing with the flour mixture. Pour milk over all to cover and sprinkle with the Parmesan cheese. Bake for 1½ hours at 350°F, until the vegetables are very tender and the gratin is golden brown. If the top browns too quickly, cover it loosely with foil. Let stand 15 minutes before serving, or better yet, make the day before and reheat.

CHICKEN POT PIE

Adapted from the *Herb Companion* magazine.

3 Tablespoons butter

½ cup diced celery

½ cup diced onion

1 small bay leaf

3 Tablespoons flour

1½ cups chicken stock

1½ cups milk

Dash or two of Tabasco sauce and Worcestershire sauce

Salt and pepper to taste

1 to 2 cups shredded or diced cooked chicken

¾ pound potatoes, diced and cooked

2 to 3 carrots, diced and cooked

4 to 6 ounces frozen peas or edamame

½ cup chopped parsley

In a large saucepan, melt the butter over low heat. Add the celery, onion and bay leaf. Cover and cook until the vegetables are soft. Sprinkle the flour over the vegetables. Stir well and cook for 5 minutes. Stir in the stock and milk. Cook, stirring occasionally, until the sauce thickens, about 15 minutes. Remove the bay leaf, add the Tabasco and Worcestershire, and season with salt and pepper. Stir in the chicken, potatoes, carrots, peas and parsley. Keep warm while you make the Biscuit Dough.

Transfer the filling to a 3-quart oven-proof casserole. Drop the dough over the filling with a large spoon, spacing it evenly to make about 6 biscuits. Bake for 20 to 25 minutes, until the biscuits are lightly browned and the pie is bubbling. Serve hot.

BISCUIT DOUGH

1 cup unbleached white flour (or use half whole wheat flour)

1½ teaspoons baking powder

¼ teaspoon salt

3 Tablespoons cold butter

½ cup milk

3 Tablespoons chopped dill

Preheat the oven to 425°F. Sift the flour, baking powder and salt together into a bowl. Cut in the butter using a knife or pastry blender. Work until the chunks are the size of peas. Add the milk and dill and stir for a minute or until the dough leaves the sides of the bowl. It will be a bit sticky.

ENGLISH SHEPHERD'S PIE

Contributed by Barb Shaw of Eugene. Barb says this is popular pub fare in Britain. And it is a great way to use leftover mashed potatoes and any local vegetables that happen to be in season.

2 cups cooked mashed potatoes

1 cup chopped fresh or frozen vegetables

1 cup leftover chicken or other meat

½ cup plain yogurt or sour cream

1 teaspoon dill weed

Salt and pepper to taste

BISCUIT BATTER FOR CRUST

1 cup flour

1 teaspoon baking powder

2 Tablespoons canola oil

¼ teaspoon salt

½ teaspoon each: thyme, rosemary and parsley

¼ cup grated cheese

⅓ cup milk

Preheat the oven to 350°F. Layer the mashed potatoes in the bottom of a baking or pie dish. Add the vegetables and meat, then a layer of yogurt or sour cream, and the dill and salt and pepper. In a separate bowl, mix the biscuit crust ingredients together, adding the milk slowly as a dough forms. Add more flour or liquid as needed. Shape the dough with your hands and lay it on top of the pie. Bake the pie for 45 minutes, until the top is golden.

PASTA WITH SAUSAGES AND GREENS

4 sausages of your choice (sweet Italian are good, but there are many hand-made sausages of various types that would suit here)

1 very large bunch of winter greens of your choice, cut into ribbons

4 to 5 cloves garlic, minced

3 Tablespoons olive oil, or more to taste

Pinch red pepper flakes

Salt and pepper to taste

½ cup or more reconstituted dried tomatoes, chopped

¼ cup chopped parsley

½ pound pasta—whole wheat is good, in whatever shape you prefer

¼ cup toasted pine nuts toasted, or toasted and chopped hazelnuts

Parmesan cheese for grating

Put up a pot of water to boil for the pasta. In a frying pan, place the sausages in an inch of water and bring to a gentle boil. Poke them with a fork a few times so they don't burst. Cook the sausages until the water evaporates, turning them a few times. Turn the heat down and brown the sausages on all sides. Remove and cut into rounds.

When the pasta water comes to a boil, add the pasta to the pot. Meanwhile, add the olive oil and garlic to the frying pan and sauté for a few minutes. Add the greens, in batches, and sauté until they are tender—5 to 10 minutes, depending on which greens you use. Add the tomatoes, red pepper flakes, salt and pepper, and parsley. Return the sausages to the pan and add a ladleful of the pasta water. When done, drain the pasta and place it in a large bowl. Pour the greens and sausages over the pasta. Grate Parmesan cheese over the top. Pass more cheese at the table.

This recipe is infinitely variable. It is good with broccoli in the fall and with zucchini in the summer. If the weather is not inclement, or even if it is, grill the sausages outside.

THE MID-WINTER VEGETABLE CURE

Adapted from *The Greens Cookbook*, Deborah Madison.

It's February and the warmth of spring seems a long way off. You've had your fill of stews and casseroles, eaten your share of hearty slaws, and now you are hungering for something fresh and light. You could buy a bag of mixed greens and get your salad fix… or you could indulge in the Mid-Winter Vegetable Cure!

Go get a load of carrots, beets, turnips, potatoes, fennel bulb, kohlrabi and whatever else suits your fancy. Cut them up into manageable sizes and steam, blanch or bake each vegetable as its nature dictates, then allow them to cool to room temperature. Arrange the medley in a lovely composition on your best platter, and pass the Parsley Sauce for your guests to ladle on top of their chosen vegetables. Serve with some crusty bread and fresh goat cheese. Life will start looking up.

PARSLEY SAUCE

3 small or 2 large cloves garlic

½ teaspoon salt

¼ teaspoon ground pepper

½ teaspoon whole fennel seeds

½ teaspoon dried tarragon

1 cup parsley

Peel of one organic lemon, grated

1 to 2 Tablespoons juice from the same lemon

1 cup olive oil

Vinegar to taste

In a food processor, whirl together the garlic, salt, pepper, fennel seeds and tarragon. Add the parsley, lemon peel and olive oil and process until well blended. Allow the dressing to sit while you prepare the vegetables. Just before serving, add vinegar to taste (red or white, as you wish). Makes about 1 cup of sauce.

MASHED RUTABAGA

Adapted from *Kitchen of Light*, Andreas Viestad.

2 pounds rutabaga, peeled and cut into 1½ inch cubes

½ pound carrots, peeled and cut into 1½ inch pieces

½ pound potatoes, peeled and cut into 1½ inch cubes

1 to 2 Tablespoons butter

¼ teaspoon grated nutmeg

In a large pot, bring 3 quarts of water to a boil. Add the rutabaga, carrots and potatoes. Cook over medium heat for 25 to 30 minutes, until the rutabaga is soft. Drain well. Mash with a potato masher or blend in a food processor until smooth. Add the butter, nutmeg, and season with salt and pepper to taste. This is a traditional Norwegian dish.

POTARROTS

My husband's recipe.

5 large potatoes (peeled or not, as you wish)

5 large carrots (ditto)

Butter, salt and pepper to taste

Chop the carrots into 2- to 3-inch chunks. Put the carrots and potatoes in a large pot, cover with water, and boil as you would for mashed potatoes. When the potatoes are done and the carrots are very tender, drain and mash with a potato masher. Add butter and salt and pepper to taste. If you want to make your Potarrots very fancy, put the mash in a baking dish, sprinkle with grated cheddar cheese, and bake uncovered at 350°F, until the cheese is melted and bubbling.

CAULIFLOWER WITH CUMIN AND CHEESE

Contributed by Hey Bales! Farm in Lorane, Oregon.

4 cups cauliflower, cut into bite-sized pieces

1 cup thinly sliced onions

¾ teaspoon whole cumin seeds

3 Tablespoons vegetable oil

1 Tablespoon cider vinegar

1 clove garlic, minced

1 cup mild white cheese, cubed (jack or something similar)

Salt and pepper to taste

Steam the cauliflower until tender. Refresh under cold water. Transfer to a serving bowl. Sauté the onions and cumin seeds in oil over medium heat, until the onions are very soft. Season with salt and pepper to taste. Combine all ingredients. Toss gently and taste for seasonings. Serve chilled.

DAVE'S SAVORY COLLARD GREENS

2 Tablespoons olive oil

1 to 2 onions, chopped

4 cloves garlic, minced

½ teaspoon crushed red pepper flakes

5 pounds collard greens

2 cups chicken stock or water, or more as needed

Salt and pepper to taste

Cider vinegar

Clean the collard greens, remove the stems and cut the leaves into ribbons. In a large pot, sauté the onions over low heat until they start to brown and smell rich. Add the garlic and red pepper and sauté for another minute. Add the collard greens, in batches, stirring until they begin to wilt. When all the greens are in, add the chicken stock or water. Bring to a boil and reduce to a simmer. Cook 40 minutes or more, until soft, adding more stock or water if necessary. When done the greens should be tender, but not mushy. Season with salt and pepper and cider vinegar to taste.

Variations: You can substitute turnip greens or mustard greens, in which case the cooking time will be much less. You can also start by cooking a bit of bacon and then adding the onions to that (in which case you won't need the olive oil).

FARM-STYLE BRAISED KALE

Contributed by Lynne Fessenden.

2 Tablespoons olive oil

½ red onion, finely chopped

2 cloves garlic, minced

1 large bunch of kale

1 Tablespoon red wine vinegar

Salt and pepper to taste

Parmesan or feta cheese (optional)

Rinse the kale, remove the stems and roughly chop the leaves. Heat the oil in a large skillet. Add the onions and garlic and cook for 6 minutes, until very soft. Stir in the kale. Add the vinegar, place a lid on the skillet, and steam for 5 to 8 minutes. Add salt and pepper to taste. Sprinkle with Parmesan or feta if desired. Replace the lid to let the cheese soften before serving.

ROASTED PARSNIPS

Contributed by Lynne Fessenden.

1 pound parsnips, peeled and cut into 3 x ½ inch sticks

2 Tablespoons olive oil

1 teaspoon oregano

½ teaspoon salt

¼ teaspoon black pepper

Preheat the oven to 375°F. Place the parsnips in a large bowl. Add the oil, oregano, salt and pepper. Toss to coat well. Place on a baking sheet. Roast for 40 minutes, turning occasionally, until the parsnips are tender and slightly browned.

CARROTS WITH GINGER AND CARDAMOM

Carrots are such an easy vegetable to come by and they are good so many ways—cut up for crudités, grated into a salad, as a main component in soup. But they can also stand alone as a side dish, and are amenable to being treated with a variety of seasonings. Here is one example.

2 Tablespoons butter

½ cup minced onion

1 inch chunk of fresh ginger root, minced

4 whole cardamom pods

1 clove garlic, minced

1½ pounds carrots, peeled and cut into rounds

1 cup chicken broth or water

Melt the butter in a medium-size skillet over medium heat. Add the onion, ginger, cardamom pods and garlic. Cook until the onion is soft. Add the carrots and stir to coat. Add the chicken broth or water. Bring to a boil. Reduce to medium low heat, cover and simmer until just tender, about 8 minutes. Uncover, increase the heat to high, and cook until the sauce thickens and glazes the carrots, stirring occasionally, about 5 minutes. Season with salt and pepper to taste.

CARROT AND TURNIP PANCAKES

Adapted from *The Cook's Garden*, Shepherd and Ellen Ogden.

4 small potatoes, scrubbed and quartered

5 carrots, cut into 1-inch chunks

1 large turnip, peeled and cut into 1-inch chunks

2 Tablespoons butter

¼ cup milk

¼ cup flour

¼ cup grated Parmesan cheese

1 Tablespoon minced fresh parsley

1 egg, beaten

Place the potatoes in a large pot and cover with water. Bring to a boil and cook until the potatoes are quite tender, about 25 minutes. During the last 10 minutes, add the carrots and turnips. Drain the vegetables, then mash them with a potato masher or process them briefly in a food processor. Transfer to a large bowl and add the butter, milk, flour, cheese, egg and parsley. Mix well. Form into small pancakes, about ½-inch thick. Sauté in a skillet with a small amount of oil, until golden brown on both sides.

SRI LANKAN CABBAGE

Reprinted from *This Organic Life*, by Joan Dye Gussow, and used with the permission of Chelsea Green Publishing. Joan originally got this recipe from a Sri Lankan gentleman.

2 onions, thinly sliced

1 to 2 Tablespoons butter or olive oil

1 teaspoon tumeric

3 to 4 whole green cardamom pods

2 to 3 whole cloves

2 to 3 cloves garlic, minced

1 head cabbage, thinly sliced

Sauté the onions in the butter or olive oil in a large frying pan. Add the tumeric, cardamom pods, cloves and garlic. When the onions are soft, add the cabbage and stir-fry until tender. Salt to taste. You can remove the cardamom and cloves, or let your guests search them out.

CELERIAC AND POTATO PURÉE

Celeriac (celery root) has to be one of the more unlikely looking vegetables you will encounter in the market. Don't let its gnarly appearance put you off, though. Waiting inside that homely exterior is a lovely, delicately-flavored vegetable.

1 to 2 large celery roots (1½ pounds)

1 pound potatoes, peeled

3 cups milk

3 cups water

Salt and pepper to taste

Butter to taste

Peel the celery root (use a stainless steel knife as iron discolors the root). They are fairly thick skinned, so you will produce a good pile of peels (which the worms in your worm bin will appreciate). Cut into 2-inch cubes, and as you go, put them in some water with lemon juice to prevent them from darkening. Cut the potatoes into 2-inch chunks as well.

Bring the milk, water and salt to a boil in a large heavy saucepan. Drain the celery root and potatoes, add them to the milk, and bring to a boil. Reduce to a simmer and cook until the vegetables are tender, about 30 minutes. Drain, then purée in a food processor or food mill until smooth. Season with butter, and salt and pepper to taste. If you are feeling indulgent, substitute cream for part of the milk.

SPICY RED CABBAGE

Adapted from *From the Garden to the Table*, Monty and Sarah Don.

1 medium-size red cabbage

1 large or 2 small tart apples

2 Tablespoons butter

1 small onion, chopped

1 Tablespoon raisins

¼ cup red wine vinegar

½ cup red wine

1 to 2 Tablespoons brown sugar

8 juniper berries, crushed

¼ teaspoon grated nutmeg

Salt and pepper to taste

Remove any damaged leaves and cut the core from the cabbage. Finely shred. Peel, core and chop the apples. Melt the butter in a large heavy-bottomed saucepan. Cook the onion until it softens, then add the cabbage and apples. Cover and cook on medium-low heat for 5 minutes. Add the raisins, vinegar, wine, sugar, juniper berries, nutmeg and salt and pepper. Bring to a boil, then reduce to a simmer and cook, uncovered, for 45 minutes. Stir regularly so that the mixture does not stick to the bottom of the pot. The dish is ready when the cabbage is tender. Do not overcook or the cabbage will turn to mush.

WINTER SQUASH WITH CIDER GLAZE AND SAGE BUTTER

Adapted from *The Herb Farm Cookbook*, Terry Traunfeld.

2 pounds winter squash, such as butternut or kabocha

3 Tablespoons butter

3 Tablespoons coarsely chopped sage leaves

1½ cups fresh apple cider

1 cup water

Salt and pepper to taste

Peel the squash and cut it into 1-inch by ½-inch chunks. Melt the butter in a large skillet over low heat. Add the sage and cook until the butter just begins to turn golden but does not turn brown, about 3 minutes (it's best if you stir while the butter is cooking). Add the squash, stir to coat, then add the cider and water. Raise the heat to bring the liquid to a boil, then reduce slightly and keep it at a gentle boil until the cider has reduced to a glaze and the squash is tender, about 30 minutes. Season with salt and pepper to taste.

SUNDAY MORNING MUFFINS

Yes, you may make these on days other than Sunday. And you may substitute other fruits for those listed below. Figs, for instance, might be nice. Or perhaps you dried some strawberries last summer. If the fruit is quite hard or chewy, soak it in boiling water for a few minutes before you add it to the batter.

⅓ cup chopped dried apricots

⅓ cup raisins

⅓ cup frozen chopped cranberries

1½ cups whole wheat flour

½ cup unbleached white flour

¾ cup brown sugar

1½ teaspoons baking powder

½ teaspoon cinnamon

¼ teaspoon baking soda

¼ teaspoon salt

2 large eggs

¾ cup low-fat plain yogurt

¼ canola oil

Preheat the oven to 350°F. Coat 12 muffin tins with oil. Set aside. Combine the flours, brown sugar, baking powder, cinnamon, baking soda and salt in a large bowl. In another bowl, whisk together the eggs, yogurt and oil. Stir the wet ingredients into the dry until the dry ingredients are just moistened (mixing your muffins too much will make them more dense). Stir in the fruit. Fill the muffin tins. Bake 20 to 25 minutes, until a toothpick inserted into the center comes out clean. Cool in the pan for a few minutes, then eat promptly.

BAKED BREAKFAST PUDDING

Easy, healthy and amenable to a multitude of variations.

2 eggs

2 cups milk

1½ cups quick-cooking oats

½ cup unbleached flour

2 teaspoons baking powder

¼ teaspoon baking soda

½ teaspoon each: ground cinnamon, ginger and tumeric

¼ cup sugar

½ cup toasted walnuts or hazelnuts, chopped

½ cup dried fruit, such as cranberries, chopped dried apples, etc. Try adding a bit of crystallized ginger for extra zing.

Yogurt for topping

Fruit preserves, such as lingonberry, for topping

Preheat the oven to 350°F. In a large bowl, beat the eggs with the milk. Stir in the oatmeal. In a smaller bowl, sift together the remaining dry ingredients and add them to the eggs, milk and oatmeal. Fold in the nuts and dried fruit. Pour into a well greased 9 x 9 inch baking pan. Bake on the middle rack for 35 to 40 minutes. Serve warm, topped with yogurt and fruit preserves.

Variations: Try maple syrup instead of sugar, or use brown sugar. Substitute a multi-grain cereal (such as Bob's Red Mill) for the oatmeal. Use fresh fruit instead of dried.

FROZEN BERRY CRISP

A bit of summer in the midst of winter.

4 to 6 cups frozen berries, such as blueberries, blackberries, strawberries or raspberries

¼ cup sugar

1 cup unbleached white flour (divided)

1 Tablespoon lemon juice

¾ cup rolled oats

⅔ cup brown sugar

1 teaspoon cinnamon

½ teaspoon ground ginger

¼ teaspoon ground nutmeg

¼ teaspoon salt

7 Tablespoons chilled butter, cut into chunks

Preheat the oven to 375°F. In a large bowl, toss the berries (no need to thaw them) with the lemon juice, sugar and ¼ cup of the flour. When well mixed, transfer to a 9-inch diameter glass pie dish or casserole.

In a bowl, combine the remaining flour with the oats, brown sugar, spices and salt. Add the butter and rub with your fingers until the mixture holds together in small clumps. Sprinkle over the berry mixture.

Bake until the berries bubble thickly and the topping is golden brown—about 1 hour. Let stand 15 minutes. Serve warm or at room temperature, with or without ice cream.

MIXED FRUIT COMPOTE

Contributed by Paula Chambers. This recipe won a prize in the "How Local Can You Go" recipe contest in the January 2008 Eat Here Now potluck organized by the Willamette Farm & Food Coalition. More a set of guidelines than a recipe, it is a great example of how to pull together fresh (stored), dried and frozen fruit.

Blueberries (frozen)

Asian pears (from storage)

Brooks plums (dried)

Blackberries (frozen)

Apples (fresh and dried)

Kiwi (fresh)

Peaches (dried)

Shiro plum jelly

Combine some or all of the above fruits in a pot and cook over medium heat, until they cook down just a bit and the dried fruit softens. Stir in sweetened, condensed milk if desired to thicken the compote.

Make a crumb topping with whole wheat flour, honey, graham crackers and cinnamon, mixed with a few tablespoons of melted butter. In a casserole dish, spread the topping over the compote and bake at 350°F, until the fruit is bubbling and the topping is golden brown. Serve with ice cream.

BAKED APPLES WITH LINGONBERRIES

Adapted from *Kitchen of Light*, Andreas Viestad. Lingonberries are a relative of the cranberry and are native to northern Europe. They grow well in the Pacific Northwest and there are a few local jam makers who produce lingonberry preserves. If you can find fresh lingonberries, use them instead of preserves, but you might want to increase the sugar a bit.

4 large apples

3 Tablespoons sugar

⅔ cup (approximately) lingonberry preserves

Without cutting all the way through, remove the core from each apple, forming a hollow about an inch in diameter. Place the apples in a baking dish. Fill the apples with the lingonberry preserves and sprinkle with sugar. Bake in a 400°F oven for 45 minutes, until tender. You can spoon the resulting juices over the apples a few times while they bake. Serve warm, with heavy cream or ice cream.

SPRING · March · April · May

The true arrival of spring in the Pacific Northwest is preceded by a long, teasing dance. Early in March, daffodils open to create joyous patches of bright yellow—often just in time for a late snow. Willows adorn themselves with long strands of the palest green pearls, not caring that the winds are still sharp and raw. By the end of the month the turkey vultures reappear, back from their southern wintering grounds, gliding in slow lazy circles above the fields. The tempo increases from that point on. Cottonwood blossoms sweeten the air. Oso berry plants unfurl their delicate leaves—the first spots of the new year's green in the wild understory. By April, hummingbirds are zipping from one blooming Oregon grape to the next, and the hills, which have been cloaked in the dark green of the fir trees all winter, are freckled with spots of chartreuse where the big leaf maples, ash and other deciduous trees have leafed out. In town, the streets are a riot of hyacinth, tulips, and plum blossoms. Finally, it really is spring!

The variety of food from the garden picks up as the season settles in. In March, when spring officially begins, we are still enjoying root vegetables that have been stored all winter, as well as cabbage, kale, leeks and other hardy brassicas that have been held over in the garden. As the season moves on, however, spring salmon start running and fresh lamb comes to the market. Early greens can be sown under cover and harvested for wonderfully delicate green salads. April sees the beginning of asparagus season. Parsley plants pop up, and cilantro, chervil and chives as well, to brighten the palate.

IN MARCH AND THE FIRST PART OF APRIL LOOK FOR

Beet Greens

Cauliflower

Early Herbs, such as parsley, chervil and chives

Fava Beans

Kale Blossoms

Leeks

Mustard Greens

Radishes

Rhubarb

Salad Greens

Spinach

Sprouting/Overwintering Broccoli

Swiss Chard

LATER IN APRIL AND INTO MAY YOU CAN ALSO FIND

Artichokes

Asian Vegetables (bok choi, etc.)

Asparagus

Beets

Broccoli

Carrots

Fennel Bulbs (immature)

Green Garlic

Green Onions

New Potatoes

Peas (sugar snap and snow)

Young Turnips and Kohlrabi

Look also for spring Chinook salmon and fresh lamb. And chickens, who have stopped producing eggs during the short dark days of winter, start laying again!

SEASON FEATURES

Artichokes: Large artichokes need the outer layers of leaves peeled off, the stems trimmed and, if you like, the top third cut off (to remove the spiny tips of the leaves). Then boil or steam them until a fork can be inserted easily into the stem end. If you are boiling them, try tossing a bay leaf, a garlic clove and a few peppercorns into the pot. Smaller young artichokes can be cut in half or in quarters, the fuzzy choke, if there is any, scooped out with a spoon, and the leaf tips cut off. They can then be steamed or sautéed. There are many lovely recipes for stuffed artichokes, but when they are fresh from the garden, artichokes are so good we are never sufficiently motivated to get past a bowlful with some lemon butter or mayonnaise for dipping.

Asparagus: Take an asparagus spear in both hands and bend it until it breaks. The long end is the part you cook, the short end you feed to your worms, or if you are so inclined, peel off the tough fibrous outside and eat the inside. Asparagus really needs nothing more than a few minutes of steam until it is just tender and bright green, a squeeze of lemon juice, and a fast trip to your mouth. Or toss them with butter and lemon. Or sesame oil and some fresh grated ginger. If you add chopped asparagus to a soup or stew, add the tips toward the end of the cooking time for the best texture and flavor.

Beets and Beet Greens: Young tender beet greens are a wonderful addition to salads. Beet greens can also be steamed and tossed with butter and herbs, or sautéed with garlic and oil and tossed with some soy sauce and a drizzle of rice vinegar. Shredded raw beets can be added to green salads during the winter and spring months in lieu of tomatoes. Cook beets whole and unpeeled, either by baking, boiling or steaming. After they have cooled, the skin slips off fairly easily.

Broccoli: Don't toss the stems out! Trim off the very bottom of the broccoli, then peel the leathery outside of the stem and chop it up to cook with the flowers. The small leaves are equally delicious. Broccoli is one of the vegetables that shows up during two seasons: look for it in the spring, and again in the fall.

Green Garlic and Garlic Whistles: Green garlic is simply garlic that has not matured fully. It is juicy and full of subtle garlic flavor, but will not store for long periods of time. Garlic whistles are the flower stalks produced by the plant. They are cut off before they open in order to redirect the plant's energy to the root, resulting in larger bulbs, or so the theory goes. Garlic whistles can be minced and sautéed for a mild garlic flavor. They are particularly good with eggs.

Peas: Sugar snap peas and snow peas come on earlier in spring than shelling peas. Both can be eaten whole and are wonderful in a stir-fry. If they have "strings," remove them by tearing the stem end down the straighter side of the pea. Sugar snap peas can also be steamed or sautéed whole and tossed with butter. Later in the season, shelled peas are great with pasta. My favorite thing to do with peas, though, is to stand in front of the pea trellis and eat. In fact, I am hard pressed to come up with any pea recipes, since they so rarely make it past my garden gate.

Radishes: Young radishes can be sliced into a salad or served simply with a dish of salt in which to dip them. They are also very good on sandwiches — sliced very thin on buttered bread (especially for an afternoon tea). Larger radishes, like the long white daikon radish, can be cut into chunks and steamed and tossed with sesame oil and soy sauce, or added to a miso-based soup.

Wild Spring Greens: Before the advent of frozen foods and midwinter shipments of fresh green vegetables, folks often went a long time without fresh greens on their plates, particularly in places where winters were harsh. With the onset of spring, early wild greens provided the first "spring tonic" of the season. Today you won't find wild spring greens in the grocery store, but you might find them in the farmers market, and you certainly could grow them in your garden or go foraging yourself (perhaps with a knowledgeable companion or well-illustrated guide). Types of wild greens include:

Amaranth: Use tender young amaranth leaves in a salad, or cook as you would spinach.

Chickweed: You probably have this common weed coming up unasked for in your garden. Put a handful in your salad, where its tart flavor will wake you up!

Cress: There are a lot of varieties of cress, including curly, upland, rock and pepper cress. They run toward the spicy side flavor-wise, but a small handful perks up a salad. Or try some cress on a sandwich for a bit of spice.

Lamb's Quarters or Quelites: Use as you would Swiss chard or spinach.

Miner's Lettuce or Claytonia: This is another plant often found in the wild that is increasingly grown domestically. It is good added to a salad of fresh greens, along with a very light dressing.

Purslane: Wild purslane grows abundantly. Domesticated varieties with larger leaves are also available. Purslane is good tossed in a salad and is very, very nutritious.

Stinging Nettles: Best picked when young, they are full of vitamins and minerals. Using tongs or gloves to handle, drop a bagful of nettle leaves into a pot of boiling water for 2 minutes, then drain and chop. At this point you can treat them rather like spinach. You might make a soup, or sauté them in olive oil and serve on crostini or pizza.

FAVA BEAN CROSTINI

Fava beans can be found most of the year, but if you find them early in the spring when they are very young and tender, they don't need to be double shelled. Just boil them in a pot of water for a few minutes, until tender.

Mash the cooked beans with a fork or potato masher, stir in chopped mint (which also makes its seasonal debut in the spring), salt to taste, and maybe add a splash of good olive oil. Spread on crostini.

Of course you can make this later in the year, but remember to double shell the beans and cook them a bit longer. You could also substitute edamame for the fava beans.

TOFU PATÉ WITH SPRING HERBS

1 block firm tofu, drained

1 stalk celery, finely minced

1 carrot, grated

2 scallions or 1 small young onion, minced

¼ cup chopped assorted fresh herbs, such as parsley, chives, chervil, marjoram or oregano, dill

2 teaspoons capers

¼ cup mayonnaise

1 teaspoon Dijon mustard

Salt and pepper to taste

Mash the tofu in a bowl with a fork or potato masher. Mix in the vegetables, capers, herbs, mayonnaise and mustard. Let the pâté sit for at least half an hour, then season with salt and pepper to taste. Serve with fresh vegetables, crackers or pita chips for dipping, or on top of crostini.

THE ULTIMATE TOSSED GREEN SALAD

Fill a big bowl with as many different varieties of salad greens as you please. It is fun to include some lettuces that are ruby red, some that are curly, and some that are more toothsome like romaine. Add other greens, such as arugula, if available. Wash, dry well and tear into mouth-sized pieces. Add a large handful of whatever fresh tender herbs you have (chopped, of course): parsley, cilantro, dill, tarragon, chervil, chives. When basil is available, definitely add that. The stronger herbs, such as rosemary, thyme and oregano, are not well suited to a tossed salad. If you have some cooked potato, cube it up and toss it in. Peas are very good too. If tomatoes or cucumbers are in season, you'll want to add them as well. Grated carrot is nice. Small bits of broccoli or cauliflower work well. Thinly sliced radishes add a bit of zing. Leftover salmon? Throw it in! Add chopped hard boiled egg, good canned tuna, cooked beans such as garbanzo or kidney — you have a full meal!

When your composition is complete, toss with your favorite dressing (mine is at the top of page 91). Don't use so much dressing that your salad is swimming in it; you just want a light coating, which will stick best to the leaves if they are dry. Finally, toss well. I was taught to toss ten times for each person eating the salad. That may be an old wives tale, or it may have been a time-management technique on the part of my mother. In any case, you want the ingredients and the dressing well integrated.

ELIN'S FAVORITE SALAD DRESSING

4 Tablespoons olive oil

1 Tablespoon wine vinegar (I often use part red wine vinegar and part balsamic. White wine vinegar gives a lighter taste. If you are feeling fancy, experiment with sherry or champagne vinegar.)

1 teaspoon fresh lemon juice

1½ teaspoons Dijon mustard

1 clove garlic, bruised

Salt and freshly ground black pepper

Combine in a jar and shake well. You can squeeze the garlic clove a bit to get more juice out, or simply bruise it and let the flavor infuse the dressing. Makes enough dressing for one large salad.

BEET AND ARUGULA SALAD WITH FRESH CHÈVRE

Contributed by Groundwork Organics.

1 bunch red, gold or Chiogga beets

1 bunch arugula

Fresh chèvre cheese

Wash the beets and trim off the greens and stems. Toss the whole beets with olive oil. Transfer to a baking dish, cover with foil and bake at 375°F for 45 minutes, until tender. Allow the beets to cool, then rub off the skins with a dry paper towel or rag. You can do this ahead of time, as roasted beets store well in the refrigerator. When you are ready to assemble the salad, slice the beets thin. Gently wash and chop the arugula. In a shallow bowl or platter, spread out the arugula and layer it with the sliced beets and crumbled chèvre. Dress with your favorite vinaigrette and ground pepper.

FAVA BEAN SALAD

Another way to enjoy fava beans in the spring—or any other time.

1 cup shelled fava beans (about 2 cups of pods)

1 Tablespoon lemon juice

1 to 2 cloves garlic, minced

2 Tablespoons extra virgin olive oil

2 teaspoons chopped mint

2 teaspoons chopped parsley

Salt and pepper to taste

¼ pound good Parmesan cheese, or substitute pecorino Romano

Lettuce

Shuck, blanch and peel the fava beans. In a small bowl, whisk the lemon juice and garlic together, then whisk in the olive oil, mint and parsley. In a large salad bowl, toss the beans with the vinaigrette and season to taste with salt and pepper. Grate cheese over the top.

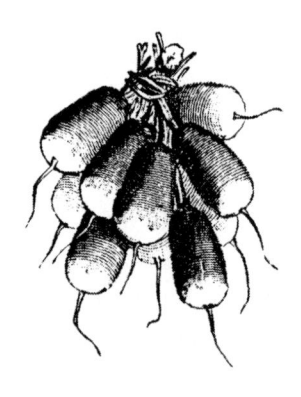

BABY BEET SALAD

¼ cup lemon juice

1 Tablespoon red wine vinegar

½ cup olive oil, plus ¼ cup extra

2 cups torn chunks of chewy bread (a good loaf of whole wheat sourdough works well)

4 ounces goat cheese

¼ cup chopped fresh herbs, such as parsley, rosemary, etc.

2 cloves garlic, minced

2 dozen baby beets, trimmed and scrubbed

1 big bowl of mixed baby greens

Preheat the oven to 375°F. Whisk together the lemon juice, vinegar and ½ cup olive oil. Season with salt and pepper to taste. Set aside.

Heat the remaining ¼ cup olive oil in an oven-proof skillet. Add the herbs and garlic. Add the bread pieces, toss to coat, and sauté until crisp. Remove the bread and toss the beets into the skillet. Cover the skillet with foil and transfer to the oven. Roast until the beets are tender, about 45 minutes. Let cool. Peel if desired (you can eat the skins of baby beets).

Toss the greens with dressing, then top with the roasted beets, goat cheese and bread chunks.

SPRING SALADS

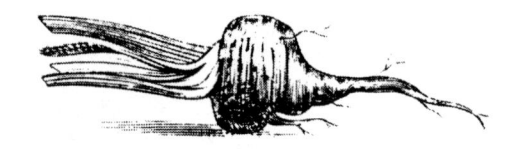

WHEAT BERRY SALAD WITH FRESH PEAS

1 cup wheat berries

6 Tablespoons olive oil

1 teaspoon grated lemon peel

1 large clove garlic, minced

1 fennel bulb

1 cup shelled fresh green peas

2 to 3 Tablespoons minced parsley

To cook the wheat berries, bring 4 cups of water to a boil, add the wheat berries and reduce heat to low. Simmer, covered for 1 hour, until the grains are tender, adding more water as needed. Cool in the covered pan. Drain if water remains in the pot.

Trim the fennel bulb and chop fine. Combine the fennel with the wheat berries, peas and parsley. Whisk together the olive oil and lemon peel. Pour the dressing over all and toss to combine. Season with salt and pepper to taste.

Variations: Carrot bits are a nice addition, as are small pieces of steamed asparagus.

CREAM OF ASPARAGUS SOUP

1 Tablespoon butter

4 ounces shallots, minced

2 cloves garlic, minced or pressed

2 pounds asparagus, tough ends removed

½ pound potatoes, cut into ½-inch cubes (leave the peels on young potatoes)

2 Tablespoons parsley, minced

½ cup dry white wine or vermouth

3 cups chicken or vegetable stock

1 teaspoon salt

½ teaspoon pepper

½ cup cream or milk

Grated Parmesan cheese (optional)

Melt the butter in a soup pot over medium heat. Add the shallots and garlic and sauté until tender but not brown. Cut the asparagus into 1-inch pieces, reserving the tips for a garnish. Add the asparagus, parsley and potato to the pot and cook for 5 minutes, until the asparagus is bright green. Add the wine and chicken or vegetable stock and simmer for 20 minutes, until the asparagus and potatoes are soft. Purée using a food processor, immersible blender or food mill. Return to the stove and stir in the cream or milk. Season to taste with salt and pepper. Garnish with lightly steamed asparagus tips and a bit of grated Parmesan cheese, if desired.

POTATO LEEK SOUP

3 Tablespoons butter or oil

1 large onion, diced

3 to 4 leeks, trimmed, halved lengthwise, washed well and sliced

2 cloves garlic, minced

1½ pounds potatoes, quartered lengthwise and sliced (peel them if you prefer)

2 to 4 cups chicken or vegetable stock

¼ teaspoon ground ginger

¼ teaspoon ground nutmeg

½ cup milk or cream

Salt and pepper to taste

Chopped arugula or sorrel for garnish

Heat the butter or oil in a soup pot. Add the onions, leeks and garlic, tossing to coat. Cover and sweat the vegetables over medium-low heat, stirring occasionally, until soft, about 20 minutes. Add the potatoes, broth, ginger and nutmeg, and bring to a boil. Reduce to a simmer and cook, partially covered, until the potatoes are very tender, about half an hour. Remove from heat and mash with a potato masher or purée in a food processor or an immersible blender (depending on how silky you like your soup). Add the milk or cream. Thin with additional stock if desired. Season with salt and pepper to taste. Just before serving, return to a simmer and scatter chopped arugula or sorrel over the surface. Cover and cook until just wilted, about 2 minutes.

GREEN RICE

Based on a casserole that my grandmother loved to take to potluck suppers, but with a few healthy twists.

3 eggs

⅔ cup milk

2 Tablespoons butter or olive oil

1 small onion, minced

2 cloves garlic, minced

3 Tablespoons brewer's yeast

¼ cup chopped fresh parsley

2 to 3 Tablespoons chopped fresh or dried dill

¼ teaspoon ground nutmeg

1 teaspoon salt

Dash of Worcestershire sauce

3 cups cooked brown Basmati rice

1½ pounds fresh spinach, washed, destemmed, and roughly chopped

2 cups grated cheese (sharp cheddar is nice)

In a large frying pan, sauté the onion in butter or olive oil until soft. Add the garlic and brewer's yeast and sauté another two or three minutes. Add the spinach in batches until all is wilted. In a large bowl, beat the eggs and milk until blended. Add the parsley, dill, nutmeg, salt and Worcestershire sauce. Fold in the spinach mixture, 1 cup cheese and the rice. Turn into a 4-quart oiled casserole dish and bake, uncovered, at 350°F for 45 minutes. Sprinkle the remaining cup of cheese over the top and bake until the cheese melts, about 5 minutes longer.

Variation: If fresh spinach is unavailable, frozen spinach is quite acceptable. Defrost it, squeeze the liquid out, and add directly to the egg and milk mixture.

ASPARAGUS WITH MUSHROOMS AND RICE

3 cups cooked brown rice

1 pound fresh asparagus

2 Tablespoons olive oil

1 onion, chopped

3 cloves garlic, minced

1 teaspoon chopped fresh dill

1 teaspoon chopped thyme

4 cups sliced mushrooms

2 Tablespoons lemon juice

½ teaspoon salt

1 teaspoon tamari

Cheddar Dijon Sauce

Trim the asparagus and cut into ½-inch pieces. Steam until barely tender.

Preheat the oven to 375°F. In a skillet, heat the oil and sauté the onion until it begins to soften. Add the garlic and thyme, and sauté a few more minutes. Add the mushrooms and sauté until they are tender. Stir this mixture into the rice. Add the dill, then add the asparagus, lemon juice, salt and tamari. Turn into a 9 x 13 inch baking dish.

Pour Cheddar Dijon Sauce over the casserole. Bake 15 minutes, until heated through.

CHEDDAR DIJON SAUCE

3 Tablespoons butter

3 Tablespoons flour

1½ cups milk

1 cup grated sharp cheddar

2 teaspoons Dijon mustard

½ teaspoon chopped dill

Melt the butter in a saucepan. Add the flour and cook for a few minutes. Add the milk and stir until it is smooth and begins to thicken. Add the cheese and stir until melted. Season with mustard and dill.

SPRING FRITTATA

Frittata is an Italian omelette. Instead of folding the eggs over to enclose the filling, however, the filling is mixed into the eggs. It is a wonderful thing for breakfast, brunch or supper, and leftovers make a great snack the next day. When made with freshly laid eggs from chickens who are responding to the lengthening days, it is a true celebration of spring.

1 Tablespoon olive oil

3 to 4 potatoes

½ cup chopped onion

2 cloves garlic

¼ teaspoon salt

5 eggs

Freshly ground pepper

1 cup packed arugula leaves

3 ounces goat cheese

Heat the olive oil in a 10-inch oven-proof skillet. Cut the potatoes into 1-inch cubes (if they are new or thin-skinned you don't need to peel them) and add them to the pan along with the onion, garlic and salt. Cook, stirring over moderate heat, until the onions are soft. Cover the pan and cook another 5 minutes or so, until the potatoes are tender.

Whisk the eggs in a small bowl and season with a pinch of salt and pepper. Coarsely chop the arugula and stir it into the eggs. Pour the mixture evenly over the potatoes and onions, but don't stir. Continue cooking until the eggs are set around the edges but still soft in the center. Sprinkle with goat cheese and place under the broiler until the frittata is puffy and golden and the cheese is somewhat melted.

Remove from broiler and loosen by sliding a rubber spatula around the sides. I serve frittata from the pan at the table, but you can also slide the whole frittata, cheese side up, onto a serving platter.

LENTILS WITH BUTTER AND PARSLEY

Adapted from *The Classic Italian Cookbook*, Julia Della Croce. This is a wonderfully simple dish that is well complemented by a large salad or platter of steamed vegetables.

½ pound brown lentils, rinsed and drained

1 large bay leaf

1 small bunch of parsley stems, tied together

3 large cloves garlic, cut in half

3 Tablespoons butter, softened

Juice of ½ lemon

3 Tablespoons finely chopped flat-leaf parsley

Salt and pepper to taste

Place the lentils in a pan with 4 cups water, the bay leaf, parsley stems and garlic. Bring to a boil, then simmer over medium-low heat, until the lentils are tender but not falling apart, about 25 minutes. Drain and discard the parsley stems, bay leaf and garlic. Meanwhile, beat the butter in a bowl until creamy. Blend in the lemon juice and 1 tablespoon of the chopped parsley. Mix the parsley butter into the hot lentils, tossing gently. Season with salt and pepper to taste. Sprinkle the remaining parsley over the lentils. Serve warm or hot. Pass extra lemon wedges and/or good olive oil to drizzle over the top of each serving.

NORTHWEST NOODLES

1 pound salmon steak or fillet

Lemon slices

¼ cup fresh chopped herbs, such as dill, parsley or chives

1 Tablespoon butter

Salt and pepper to taste

White wine

1 package pasta of your choice—penne, radiatore, fusilli, etc.

1 large bunch chard, cut into ribbons

3 to 4 cloves garlic, minced

2 to 3 Tablespoons olive oil

1 cup roasted hazelnuts, chopped

½ cup dried tomatoes, softened in boiling water, or drained of oil, and diced

Parmesan cheese

Place the salmon in an 8 x 8 inch baking dish. Cut up the butter and scatter it over the fish. Sprinkle with chopped herbs and salt and pepper to taste. Top with lemon slices. Add wine so that there is a ½-inch of liquid. Bake at 400°F for 10 minutes, until the fish flakes easily with a fork. Cool, remove skin, and break into chunks. Alternatively, use leftover salmon.

Bring a pot of water to a boil and cook the pasta. While the pasta cooks, heat olive oil in a large frying pan and add the garlic. Sauté for a minute, then add the greens and cook until they are tender but not mushy. Add the salmon, dried tomatoes and hazelnuts. Toss gently and remove from heat. When the pasta is done, mix it with the greens/salmon mixture and sprinkle liberally with freshly grated Parmesan.

Variation: If you like things a bit saucier, add some of the pasta water to the greens mixture just before tossing it with the pasta.

PASTA WITH KALE "RABE" AND TUNA

In the spring, kale plants start going to flower. When it flowers, the stalks lengthen, the leaves change shape, and both become quite tender and sweet. If you get out into the garden and cut the blossoms as they are just forming—when they look like broccoli rabe (also known as rapini, broccoli raab, broccoletti di rape and broccoletto) —they are quite tasty. In fact, the word rabe is from the Latin and literally means "flowering tops of turnips." Kale rabe is not something that you find often in a grocery store, but I have seen the flower stalks bundled for sale in farmers markets.

1 pound kale rabe, chopped

2 Tablespoons olive oil

½ cup sun-dried tomatoes, drained of oil or soaked in boiling water if dry, and chopped

8 ounces whole wheat pasta

½ cup pine nuts, toasted
(or substitute walnuts, or even toasted hazelnuts)

4 to 6 cloves garlic

1 can line-caught tuna

¼ cup chopped parsley

Parmesan cheese to taste

Lemon juice

Cook the pasta. While it is cooking, heat the oil and sauté the garlic briefly. Add the kale and sauté until it is bright green and just tender. Add the pine nuts and tomatoes. Mix with the cooked pasta and add the tuna and parsley. Squeeze some lemon juice over it, drizzle with more olive oil if desired, and top with grated Parmesan to taste.

Variation: When in season, substitute asparagus for the kale rabe.

JAKE'S TOFU-TURKEY PIE

Jake Walsh is our Buddhist builder. Tofu-Turkey Pie is a staple at his house.

½ pound turkey breakfast sausage

3 leeks, sliced, or ½ onion, minced

4 cloves garlic, minced

2 carrots, minced

½ cup fresh or frozen peas, or 1 small head broccoli, cut into small pieces

1 block firm tofu

½ cup cottage cheese

4 eggs, beaten

½ cup milk

½ cup grated cheese, such as mozzarella, cheddar, or whatever you have on hand

1 teaspoon nutmeg

Salt and pepper to taste

2 pie shells

Brown the sausage and set aside. Sauté the leeks or onion and garlic in oil or butter until soft. Add the carrots, peas or broccoli, and cook until just tender. Add the meat back to the pan. In a bowl, mash the tofu and mix with the cottage cheese and grated cheese. Combine the cheeses and tofu with the vegetables and meat and fill the 2 pie shells. Mix the eggs and milk and pour half over each pie. Bake at 350°F for 45 minutes, until a knife inserted into the center comes out clean.

Jake's Variations: Make it Tex-Mex by adding beans and diced green chiles, then seasoning with cumin and cilantro. Or go Greek by substituting ground lamb for the sausage, spinach for the carrots and peas, and seasoning with oregano. For a vegetarian variation try vegetarian sausage patties.

SPINACH WITH SESAME DRESSING (HORENSO NO GOMA-AE)

This is good when made with the first very tender spinach leaves of the spring, which are similar to the spinach grown in Japan. The combination of soy sauce, sugar and sesame seeds is fairly addicting.

1 pound fresh young spinach plants, washed but roots kept intact

4 Tablespoons sesame seeds

1 teaspoon sugar

2 teaspoons soy sauce

3 Tablespoons chicken stock

After washing the plants, drop them briefly into a pot of boiling water, until just limp. Remove and rinse under cold running water to stop the cooking process. Gently squeeze the extra moisture out of the leaves. Cut off the stems and roots and discard. Roughly chop the leaves and set aside.

Toast the sesame seeds in a dry frying pan over medium heat until the seeds are golden — watch them closely and shake frequently so they don't burn. Crush the hot seeds in a Japanese suribachi or with a mortar and pestle. Add the sugar and stir. Add the soy sauce and stock and blend very well. Taste and add a bit more sugar if you think it needs it, but don't make it too sweet. Mix the dressing gently with the spinach. Serve at room temperature.

SPRING SIDE DISHES

GINGER-MARINATED ASPARAGUS

Adapted from *Still Life with Menu*, Mollie Katzen.

¾ cup cider vinegar or unseasoned rice vinegar

2 Tablespoons sugar

2 Tablespoons grated fresh ginger

1 pound fresh asparagus

1 clove garlic, minced or pressed

2 Tablespoons toasted sesame oil

3 Tablespoons canola oil

½ teaspoon salt

1 teaspoon soy sauce

In a small saucepan, combine the vinegar and ginger and bring to a boil. Cook uncovered over medium heat until the mixture is reduced by half—about 15 minutes. Remove from heat, add the sugar and set aside.

Steam the asparagus until just tender and still bright green. Remove from pan and immerse in cold water to stop the cooking process. Drain, let them dry a bit, then arrange on a platter.

Combine the garlic, oils, salt and soy sauce and pour the mixture over the asparagus, tossing gently to coat. Drizzle the vinegar-ginger mix on top and let the dish rest an hour before serving. Delicious at either room temperature or chilled.

KOHLRABI FRITTERS WITH FRESH HERBS

Contributed by Sweetwater Farm in Creswell, Oregon.

1 large or 2 small kohlrabi, peeled and grated to make 2 cups

1 teaspoon baking powder

2 Tablespoons chopped sage blossoms

2 Tablespoons Parmesan cheese

1 large or 2 medium eggs

3 Tablespoons finely minced onion or shallot

1 or more cloves garlic, minced

Salt and pepper to taste

Oil for frying

2 Tablespoons flour

Combine the kohlrabi with the onion and garlic. Mix well. Sprinkle with the flour, baking powder and Parmesan cheese and mix again. Beat the eggs with salt and pepper and stir them into the kohlrabi mixture. Add the herbs and toss lightly. Heat an oiled griddle. For each fritter, drop 2 tablespoons of batter onto the hot griddle and flatten to a uniform thickness. Cook about 2 minutes on each side, until golden brown. Serve hot.

Note: This could be made in the fall and winter too, but without the sage blossoms. Other fresh herbs that might work in place of sage blossoms are dill, sage leaves, garlic chives or chervil.

ROAST BEETS WITH THYME AND GARLIC

6 small beets

3 small whole bulbs garlic, cut in half horizontally

1 large bunch fresh thyme

Salt

Olive oil

Wash the beets and chop off the tops, but leave the skin intact. Quarter them and arrange in a roasting dish surrounded by the halved garlic bulbs. Scatter thyme branches over the beets, sprinkle with salt and olive oil, and toss a bit to make sure the beets are coated with oil. Roast at 375°F for 35 to 40 minutes. Serve hot, with bread, onto which the garlic can be spread.

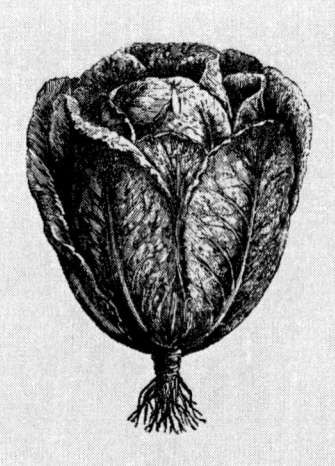

RHUBARB CRISP

5 cups diced rhubarb

1 cup sugar

Grated rind of 1 orange

3 Tablespoons corn starch, dissolved into ½ cup water

1 teaspoon vanilla

TOPPING

1 cup rolled oats

½ cup unbleached white flour

½ cup brown sugar

½ teaspoon cinnamon

½ teaspoon ground ginger

⅛ teaspoon salt

½ cup cold butter, cut into chunks

Mix the rhubarb, sugar, orange and corn starch together in a large saucepan. Cook until thickened. Add the vanilla. Pour into a shallow 2- to 3-quart baking dish.

In a large bowl, mix the oats, flour, sugar, spices and salt. Mix in the butter with your fingers or a pastry blender until coarse crumbs form. Sprinkle evenly over the filling. Bake at 350°F, until the topping is golden brown and the filling is bubbling, about 45 minutes. Serve warm or at room temperature, topped, if you like, with cream, ice cream or yogurt.

RHUBARB SAUCE

Rhubarb is one of the first "fruits" of the season, although, of course, it is not a fruit at all, but a vegetable that is, oddly enough, a member of the buckwheat family.

2 cups diced rhubarb (about 1 pound)

½ cup sugar

¼ cup water

Dash of ground cinnamon and/or nutmeg

Heat the rhubarb, sugar and water in a saucepan over medium heat, until the mixture thickens, about 10 minutes. Season with cinnamon or nutmeg and serve warm on top of ice cream.

MARIJO'S RHUBARB CAKE

Contributed by Marijo Taylor.

½ **cup butter, room temperature**

1 cup sugar, plus 2 Tablespoons for topping

1 large egg

1 teaspoon vanilla

1 cup buttermilk

1 teaspoon baking soda

2 cups flour

1 ½ to 2 cups finely chopped rhubarb

1 teaspoon cinnamon

In a large bowl, cream the butter and sugar. Add the egg, vanilla and buttermilk. Beat well. In a smaller bowl, sift the baking soda and flour together. Add the flour mixture to the wet ingredients and stir until just moistened.

Pour the batter into a greased 8 x 8 inch cake pan. Dust the top with a mixture of 2 tablespoons of sugar plus the cinnamon. Bake at 350°F for 40 minutes, until a toothpick inserted into the center comes out clean.

SUMMER · June · July · August

Ahh, June. The kids are out of school. The days are warm enough to truly warrant shorts and sandals. The soil has warmed enough for tomatoes and basil to be happy about being set out in the garden. And in the farmers market the stands are bursting with long golden carrots, crunchy fresh peas, piles of lettuce in a myriad of colors. From some booths the tantalizing aroma of early tomatoes ripened on the vine under cover pulls us in as surely as a Siren's song. Children wander about with strawberry-tinted grins on their faces, and later in the month, if the weather has been good, the first blueberries appear. It is a time of gastronomic delight!

Summer is an easy time to eat seasonally. The variety of available fruits and vegetables increases almost daily. It is also a time to start putting up food that has been locally grown—by freezing, drying or canning—to use during the rest of the year. And if you are growing your own food, it is time to plant winter crops—they need time to get established before the sun loses its strength.

Although we typically think of it as one season, summer really has two distinct parts: early summer, which still has one foot in spring; and late summer, which has an eye already toward fall. The foods we typically associate with summer, such as corn, tomatoes, melons, peaches, and peppers, are usually not found until late summer, and in some years, they don't really come into their own until the kids go back to school in September. June, on the other hand, is still filled with tender lettuces, shelling peas, artichokes, broccoli, and oriental greens such as bok choi and Chinese cabbage.

IN JUNE AND JULY, LOOK FOR

Blueberries

Broccoli

Cabbage

Cauliflower

Cherries

Edamame

Green Beans

Herbs, such as Dill, Cilantro, Mint, Parsley and Chives

Lettuce

Peas (shelling)

Potatoes

Strawberries

Summer Squash

Sweet Onions

LATER, IN JULY AND AUGUST, YOU WILL ALSO FIND

Apples (early varieties)

Basil

Berries of all kinds

Corn

Cucumber

Early Apples

Eggplant

Garlic

Melons

Peaches

Pears

Peppers

Plums

Storage Onions

Tomatillos

Tomatoes

SEASON FEATURES

Beans: Green beans are best when they are just starting to plump up. Picked fresh or purchased at a farmers market and sent straight to the kitchen, there is nothing better than a bowl of beans steamed briefly until just tender and then tossed with butter and a bit of salt. For variety, add some toasted chopped almonds or hazelnuts, or toss with some chopped basil or summer savory. Cooked green beans can be puréed and mixed with olive oil, garlic and herbs and served on a bed of greens or as a dip. Fresh shelling beans (in other words, green beans that have matured until the pod is no longer tender, but the bean seeds inside have not yet reached the drying bean stage) such as flageolet, lima or runner beans should be simmered in stock or water until just tender. Try adding a bay leaf, some herbs such as savory, thyme and parsley, a garlic clove and half an onion to the simmering liquid for more flavorful beans.

Corn: There really is not much that can improve on an ear of corn that has been stripped off the stalk, husked, rushed to the kitchen, and deposited directly into a pot of boiling water for a minute or two and then slathered with butter and perhaps a sprinkle of salt. However, if you are inclined to try something different, soak the unhusked ears in cold water for half an hour, then grill them over a low fire for about 10 minutes, rolling them around every so often until evenly cooked. Or pull back the outer leaves, leaving just the inner ones, and bake at 375°F for 15 minutes. If you have leftover corn, scrape the kernels off the cob and freeze, or use them the next day in a frittata, a batch of cornbread, or a pot of soup.

Cucumber: Rather like summer squash and zucchini, cucumber is best when picked young before the seeds have had a chance to develop. Cucumbers make a lovely salad all by themselves, or mixed with tomatoes. Try some of the different varieties, such as lemon cucumbers and Asian cucumbers.

Eggplant: Here, too, there is a world of difference in the many varieties you can find at your farmers market (or in the seed catalog). There are green, white, and purple-striped eggplants, long skinny eggplants, small round eggplants. The elongated Japanese eggplants have a very thin skin and do not need to be peeled. The large pear-shaped eggplants are good for slicing and layering. Eggplant can be baked and then marinated in a vinaigrette. Slices of eggplant can be brushed with olive oil and grilled. Whole eggplants can be roasted at 450°F, until charred, then scooped out, puréed and mixed with lemon juice, tahini and garlic, and served as a dip. Or toss the puréed flesh with pasta and roasted garlic and peppers. Cubes of eggplant are wonderful in ratatouille or vegetable stew, or roasted with tomatoes for a pasta sauce.

Edamame: Also called sweet soybeans, edamame are a regular feature in Japanese pubs, where bowls of salted pods are served in place of pretzels. They are very easy to cook. Simply bring a pot of water to boil, add the whole pods and a couple of tablespoons of salt, and boil for 3 to 4 minutes. Drain, then toss in a bowl with a bit more salt. To eat, squeeze and pop the beans out of the pod directly into your mouth. You can also shell the beans, then blanch and freeze them on a cookie sheet to use in place of frozen peas or lima beans in soups, stews and casseroles during the winter.

Summer Squash: OK, everybody is familiar with the ubiquitous zucchini. Long green vegetables with a habit of growing out of control overnight. But have you tried the round ones that look like pool balls? Or regular zucchini when they are only as thick as your finger? Or the delicate nutty-flavored patty pan squash (the ones that look vaguely like flying saucers)? Summer squash are more than just zucchini! Squash can be sautéed with garlic, olive oil, tomatoes and fresh basil as a sort of Italian side dish. The big ones can be scooped out, stuffed with a filling and baked. Or cut large zucchini into ½-inch slabs, brush with olive oil and grill. Add summer squash to soups, stews and stir-fries. Grated squash is really good in corn bread… and, of course, there is always zucchini bread.

Tomatoes: I like my tomatoes warm from the sun, cut into thick slabs, and laid on good bread with a bit of salt, a moderate amount of mayonnaise, and a few fresh leaves of basil. Or layered on a serving dish, perhaps alternated with slices of fresh cucumber, sprinkled with chopped fresh basil, and drizzled with balsamic vinegar and good olive oil. Then again, with pasta: chop up a few ripe tomatoes and mix them with hot pasta, lots of minced garlic, and olive oil. Top with freshly grated Parmesan cheese.

Tomatillos: Tomatillos are not tomatoes. They are actually related to gooseberries (a fruit native to North America that is also covered with a papery husk) and have been a part of the diet of Mexico and Guatemala for hundreds of years. When eaten raw, they are tangy and firm to the bite. If roasted or boiled, they soften and the flavor mellows. To use, peel off the papery skin and rinse off the sticky residue. When peeled they can be stored in a plastic bag in the refrigerator for up to three months; unpeeled they will keep well in a paper bag for about a month. Chopped finely, raw tomatillos are wonderful in salsa or salad. Or toss them with some onion, garlic, an Anaheim chile (seeded) and vegetable oil, roast at 400°F, until soft and a bit charred, then purée and use in enchilada sauce.

CLAUDIA'S SUMMER CROSTINI

2 tomatoes, chopped

½ red onion, chopped

3 stalks celery, chopped

1 bell pepper, chopped

1 cup fresh basil leaves, minced

2 to 3 cloves garlic, minced, to taste

Salt and pepper to taste

½ cup olive oil

1 baguette, sliced

Combine all ingredients, except the bread, and marinate overnight. The next day, brush the sliced bread with olive oil, then broil or grill until toasted. Top with a good spoonful of the marinated vegetables and serve immediately.

EGGPLANT BRUSCHETTA

3 long slender eggplants

6 ripe Roma tomatoes or 3 large slicing tomatoes, sliced

4 ounces goat cheese or other soft cheese, such as fresh mozzarella

1 to 2 cloves garlic

6 slices of hearty bread — Italian, sourdough, whole grain

Olive oil

2 Tablespoons finely shredded fresh basil

Remove the stems from the eggplant and slice lengthwise into ¼-inch slabs. Brush both sides with olive oil and grill until just softened and lightly browned. Brush the bread with olive oil and grill or broil. Rub the toasted bread well with the garlic cloves. Layer the eggplant, sliced tomatoes, basil and cheese on the bread. Place on a covered grill or under a broiler until the cheese melts. Serve immediately. The question: Is this an appetizer or a full meal? You decide.

BILL MUMBACH'S FRESH SWEET ONION RINGS WITH BASIL

Bill Mumbach was a wonderful friend of my husband who gave us seeds for an over-wintering sweet onion known to us only as Bill's Onions. Walla Walla onions work just as well, however.

1 large sweet onion

½ cup seasoned rice vinegar (or plain rice vinegar with 1 teaspoon sugar)

1 Tablespoon minced fresh basil

⅛ teaspoon red pepper flakes

1 cup small ice cubes

Salt to taste

Cut the onions into ¼-inch thick slices and separate the rings. Combine the vinegar, basil and red pepper and pour over the onions. Top with the ice cubes and let it rest for 15 to 20 minutes. The ice cubes will melt to dilute the vinegar properly. Tastes even better the next day. Also heavenly on sandwiches.

SUMMER SALADS

Most lettuces dislike the heat of mid-summer, so while the archetypal salad is a composition of lettuce, tomato and cucumber, a more appropriate seasonal salad for high summer might be variations on a theme of tomato and cucumber.

TOMATOES LUTÈCE

Contributed by Jude Hobbs, reprinted from the Willamette Farm & Food Coalition's "Locally Grown" directory.

8 ripe tomatoes

¼ cup chopped parsley

1 clove garlic, crushed

½ teaspoon salt

1 teaspoon sugar or honey

½ teaspoon pepper

¼ cup olive oil

2 Tablespoons balsamic vinegar

2 teaspoons prepared mustard

Slice the tomatoes and place in a shallow dish. Combine all other ingredients in a small jar and shake well. Pour over the tomatoes. Let stand at room temperature for half an hour before serving.

PASTA SALAD WITH TOMATO AND FETA CHEESE

1 pound pasta of your choice—orzo is very good, fusilli is fun, gemelli works well…

¼ cup fresh lemon juice

6 teaspoons minced fresh herbs, such as parsley, mint, basil, marjoram, dill

4 teaspoons Dijon mustard

1 teaspoon grated lemon peel

½ cup olive oil

1 cup crumbled feta cheese

½ cup pitted Kalamata olives, chopped

2 cups cherry tomatoes, halved

Cook the pasta until al dente. Drain and rinse well under cold water. Transfer to a large bowl. Mix the lemon juice, herbs, mustard and lemon peel in small bowl. Whisk in the olive oil. Add the dressing, feta cheese and olives to the pasta, toss to coat, and season to taste with salt and pepper. Cover and let stand 2 hours to allow the flavors to become well acquainted. Just before serving, gently toss in the tomatoes.

FARMOR'S POTATO SALAD

My paternal grandmother (Farmor means father's mother in Swedish) passed this recipe on to my mother. I now pass it on to you.

Scrub, but don't peel, one medium potato per person. Cook until just tender but not falling apart. Drain, cool until you can handle, peel and cut into chunks. Toss with several tablespoons Potato Salad Dressing. Add a handful of chopped parsley, freshly ground pepper, some chopped onion (sweet onion is very good), chopped celery, 1 tablespoon chopped fresh marjoram and/or oregano. Toss well, cover, let chill overnight.

The next day, add some coarsely chopped pimento-stuffed green olives and enough mayonnaise to bind together. Adjust seasonings. Decorate with sliced hardboiled eggs, slices of olives and paprika.

POTATO SALAD DRESSING

2 Tablespoons balsamic vinegar

2 Tablespoons red wine vinegar

1 teaspoon Dijon mustard

1 inch anchovy paste (optional)

Pinch salt

3 to 4 twists of black pepper

5 Tablespoons olive oil

1 clove garlic, minced or pressed

½ teaspoon Worcestershire sauce

Shake well. Store in the refrigerator.

NATASHA'S VENEZUELAN BOYFRIEND'S AUNT'S GREEN SALAD

Contributed by my good friend, Marijo Taylor. Make this in mid-summer while the blueberries are abundant and the lettuce is still happy, or in the fall with apples or pears.

Compose a large bowl of:

Romaine lettuce or other assorted salad greens and spinach

Gorgonzola cheese, crumbled

Fresh blueberries

Chopped pecans, toasted or candied, or use walnuts

Dried cranberries or raisins

Dress it with:

½ cup balsamic vinegar

1 cup olive oil

1 teaspoon to 1 Tablespoon sesame oil

Salt and pepper to taste

4 cloves garlic, minced

TABBOULI

There are hundreds of ways to improvise with tabbouli. Try it with couscous or quinoa instead of bulgar wheat. Add steamed vegetables. Increase the amount of parsley and mint to make it very green. Add feta cheese and garbanzo beans to make it a complete meal.

1 cup bulgar wheat

1½ cups boiling water

1 teaspoon salt

Juice of 1 large lemon

1 large clove garlic, pressed

¼ cup olive oil

1 Tablespoon chopped fresh mint, or more to taste

1 cup chopped parsley

1 cucumber, chopped

2 to 3 medium tomatoes, chopped

½ cup feta cheese (optional)

1 cup cooked garbanzo beans, or 1 can drained (optional)

Combine the bulgar, boiling water and salt in a bowl. Cover with a plate and let stand until the bulgar has absorbed all the water and is chewy—about 20 minutes.

Mix the lemon juice, garlic, oil, mint and parsley. Toss with the bulgar wheat and refrigerate 1 to 2 hours. Before serving, toss gently with the cucumber and tomatoes, feta and garbanzos (if using). Even better the next day.

SUMMER SOUPS

GAZPACHO

Adapted from *The Moosewood Cookbook*, Mollie Katzen.

1 quart Very Veggie juice or fresh tomato juice

1 to 2 cloves garlic, pressed

¼ cup lemon juice (half a large lemon)

¼ cup lime juice (1 lime)

2 Tablespoons red wine vinegar

1 teaspoon each: minced fresh tarragon and basil

¼ teaspoon ground cumin

¼ cup chopped parsley

Dash Tabasco sauce

2 Tablespoons olive oil

1 small onion, finely minced (Walla Wallas are good)

2 cups diced fresh tomatoes

1 large green pepper, minced

1 cucumber, diced

Salt and pepper to taste

Combine all ingredients and chill for at least 2 hours. You can purée the soup if you like, but I prefer it chunky.

BAKED TOMATO SPAGHETTI

1½ to 2 pounds Roma tomatoes

3 to 6 cloves garlic, minced

½ cup chopped flat-leaf parsley

½ cup olive oil

1 pound spaghetti

2 Tablespoons butter

½ cup fresh whole basil leaves, cut into ribbons

Grated Parmesan cheese

Cut the tomatoes in half lengthwise and set, cut side up, in a 9 x 13 inch baking pan. Sprinkle lightly with salt and pepper. Mix the garlic, ⅓ cup parsley and 2 tablespoons olive oil, and pat the mixture over the cut sides of the tomatoes. Drizzle 2 more tablespoons olive oil over the tomatoes and bake at 425°F, about 50 to 60 minutes, until browned on top.

Boil the spaghetti until al dente. Drain. In a large serving bowl, combine the butter, remaining parsley and oil, basil and 4 tomato halves. Mash coarsely. Add the pasta and mix. Add the remaining tomatoes and pan juices, gently toss, adding salt and pepper and cheese to taste. Offer more cheese to grate at the table.

Note: If you make this with slicing tomatoes instead of paste tomatoes, there will be an abundance of pan juices. Mix as much of the juices into the pasta as desired, then freeze whatever is leftover in the pan to add later to a pot of soup.

RED DEVIL SQUASH CREOLE

Contributed by Wintergreen Farm in Noti, Oregon.

6 medium summer squash, cut into 1-inch chunks

3 Tablespoons butter

2 medium onions, sliced

1 red and 1 green bell pepper, cut into strips

3 Tablespoons brown sugar

3 Tablespoons flour

4 cups tomatoes, quartered

¼ pound grated sharp cheese

Salt and pepper to taste

Steam the squash until barely tender. Drain. Melt the butter in a large skillet, add the onions and pepper, sauté until soft. Sprinkle the sugar over the mixture, add the flour, stir gently. Stir in the tomatoes. Simmer a bit. Heat the oven to 350°F. Butter a large baking dish. Layer half the squash in the dish, top with half the tomato mixture. Repeat layers. Season with salt and pepper, top with cheese. Bake 30 minutes, until the cheese is bubbling.

PAD THAI

Contributed by Wintergreen Farm in Noti, Oregon.

1 pound rice noodles

1 pound tofu

2 to 3 Tablespoons olive oil

1 pound bok choi or other veggies, chopped

2 Tablespoons soy sauce

3 diced chili peppers or 3 teaspoons cayenne

2 Tablespoons chopped cilantro

2 Tablespoons chopped peanuts

SPICE PASTE

1 Tablespoon fresh lime juice

3 Tablespoons soy or fish sauce

3 Tablespoons ketchup

2 Tablespoons sugar

2 chopped onions

Pulverize the spice paste ingredients together in a food processor or mortar and pestle. Boil enough water to cover the noodles. Add the noodles to the hot water, turn off the heat and soak for 10 minutes. Drain, reserving some of the water. In a large pan or wok, sauté the tofu in the spice paste and oil for 2 minutes. Add the veggies, sauté until tender. Add the noodles, soy sauce and chili peppers or cayenne. Mix well. If the mixture needs more liquid, add some of the cooking water. Top with cilantro and peanuts.

ASIAN-STYLE HONEY GLAZED RIBS

Contributed by culinary artisan Joseph Metts, who made this for the January 2008 How Local Can You Go contest at Willamette Farm & Food's Eat Here potluck. Sweet Briar Farms of Eugene raises Duroc pigs, a heritage breed, raised without antibiotics or growth hormones.

3½ pounds or 2 racks of Sweet-Briar-Farms St. Louis or spare pork ribs

1½ cups local wildflower honey

⅔ cup minced garlic

1 small shallot, minced

⅓ cup apple cider vinegar

1 Tablespoon chili powder

½ cup sunflower seed oil or any high heat oil

⅓ cup triple sec, orange liqueur or orange juice

2 Tablespoons red pepper flakes

3 Tablespoons coriander seeds

1 Tablespoon cumin seeds

¼ cup soy sauce or tamari

3 Tablespoons peppercorns

1 leek, sliced

1 serrano pepper, minced or thinly sliced

¼ cup minced fresh ginger

⅛ teaspoon cayenne pepper, or to taste

3 Tablespoons rapidura or brown sugar

¾ cup fresh cilantro, chopped

¼ cup toasted sesame seeds

In a spice grinder or mortar, grind the coriander, cumin and peppercorns. Set aside 2 tablespoons of the mix for later. Combine the rest of the ground seeds, ¾ cup honey, garlic, shallot, vinegar, chili, oil, liqueur, pepper flakes and soy sauce. Drizzle and rub the mixture into the ribs, marinate for 2 to 4 hours (for overnight marinade use only ¼ cup of vinegar). In a high heat oven, broiler, or on a grill, sear ribs until golden brown. To make things easier for service you can cut the racks into 2 to 3 rib sections. Place the ribs in a deep dish pan. Drizzle with ¼ cup honey, add the leeks and peppers, cover, and cook in a 325 to 350°F oven, 4 to 5 hours, until the meat is tender. 30 minutes before the ribs are done, combine the rest of the honey, ginger, reserved spice mix, cayenne, sugar, and a little water in a saucepan and bring to a simmer for about 10 minutes (for hotter/milder ribs use more/less cayenne). Remove the ribs from the oven, drizzle the spicy honey glaze over them, and sprinkle with sesame seeds and cilantro. Enjoy with friends and family!

GROUNDWORK ORGANICS FAVORITE VEGGIE MELT

Good for breakfast, lunch or dinner!

Step 1: Slice about 6 well scrubbed potatoes into ¼-inch rounds. Slice an onion in half, cut it length-wise, then break it apart. Toss the potatoes and onion with olive oil and salt and pepper to taste. Spread on a greased baking sheet and bake, uncovered, at 375°F, until slightly browned, about 45 minutes.

Step 2: Prepare vegetables of your choice. Use any combination that sounds appealing: zucchini, broccoli, beans, greens, etc. Steam until just tender.

Step 3: Grate about 1½ cups of cheese (cheddar, jack, mozzarella, or a combination). On the baking sheet, layer potatoes, cheese, steamed vegetables, and a little more cheese. Melt until just golden under a hot broiler, about 3 minutes.

MEXICAN VEGGIE POT PIE

4 to 5 medium summer squash—zucchini and/or patty pan, etc.—cut into small chunks

1 onion, minced

3 to 4 cloves garlic, minced

2 Tablespoons vegetable oil

½ to 1 teaspoon whole cumin seeds

½ teaspoon oregano

1 to 2 peppers of choice, either fresh or roasted
(I use Anaheim, but you can use something with more bite)

1 can black beans, drained

1 cup grated cheddar cheese

¼ cup sour cream

1 batch Good Corn Bread

Sauté the onion in oil until the onion starts to turn golden. Add the garlic, cumin seeds, oregano and peppers. Sauté for a few more minutes—longer if you are using fresh peppers, just a few minutes for roasted. Add the squash and sauté until tender. Add the beans and the keep mixture warm while you mix the corn bread batter.

Grease a large casserole dish. Mix the cheese and sour cream and add it to the squash/bean mix. Pour into a casserole dish. Top with the corn bread batter. Bake at 400°F for 30 minutes, until the corn bread is lightly browned.

GOOD CORN BREAD

1 cup stone-ground cornmeal (Bob's Red Mill makes a good coarse grind)

1 cup unbleached white flour

1 Tablespoon baking powder

¼ teaspoon salt

¼ teaspoon baking soda

1 to 3 Tablespoons sugar (depending on how sweet you like your corn bread—are you a Yankee or a Southerner?)

1¼ cups buttermilk

1 large egg

¼ cup canola oil

Combine the dry ingredients in a large bowl. Whisk the wet ingredients together in a small bowl, then fold them into the dry mixture. Stir only enough to wet everything. Liberally butter a 7-inch cast-iron skillet or 8 x 8 inch baking pan, pour in the batter and bake 15 to 20 minutes, until golden brown. Or if making a topping for pot pie, follow the directions on page 132.

STILLPOINT FARM'S GRILLED JAPANESE EGGPLANT

1 Tablespoon minced garlic

2 Tablespoons soy sauce

1 Tablespoon rice vinegar (or balsamic)

1 Tablespoon vegetable oil

2 teaspoons sesame oil (use hot sesame oil if you like things spicy)

4 Japanese eggplant

9 green onions

Combine the first five ingredients in a bowl. Cut the eggplant lengthwise into 1-inch slices. Trim off the root ends of the green onions. Put the eggplant and onions in the marinade and let stand for 15 minutes. Cook the eggplant on a hot oiled grill for 3 minutes on each side. Then add the onions and cook for 1 minute on each side. You can also add peppers and summer squash!

MEXICAN CORN

Contributed by Hey Bales! Farm in Lorane, Oregon.

Strip the outer husks from 6 ears of corn, leaving a few inner husks attached. Remove silks. Soak the corn in cold water for about 10 minutes, drain and grill over medium heat until slightly charred on all sides. Mix about 1 tablespoon chili powder with ½ cup mayonnaise. Slice a few limes into wedges and grate some Parmesan cheese. At the table, rub the corn with a wedge of lime, spread with the mayonnaise mix, and sprinkle on the Parmesan.

RISOTTO WITH ONIONS, CARROTS AND FENNEL

Contributed by Wintergreen Farm in Noti, Oregon.

3 carrots, cut into ¼-inch cubes

1 fennel bulb, diced

3 small onions, diced

1 Tablespoon olive oil

1 cup dry rice (arborio makes good risotto)

½ cup dry white wine

1 teaspoon minced fresh thyme

¼ cup minced parsley

3 Tablespoons grated Parmesan cheese

In a medium-size saucepan, bring 4 cups water to a boil. Reduce heat to low. Clean and trim the carrots, fennel and onions. Add the trimmings to the simmering water to make a vegetable broth. In a large heavy-bottomed saucepan, sauté the vegetables in oil for two minutes. Add the rice and sauté for 2 more minutes. Add the wine and stir gently over low heat until the liquid is absorbed. Add broth ½ cup at a time, stirring until each is absorbed (strain out the trimmings first, of course). Continue adding broth and stirring until the rice is moist, but not soupy, about 20 to 30 minutes. Remove from heat, garnish with parsley, thyme and Parmesan cheese.

GREEN BEAN TOMATO CURRY

Contributed by Wintergreen Farm in Noti, Oregon.

1 Tablespoon olive oil

1 Tablespoon minced fresh ginger

1 Tablespoon cumin seeds

¾ teaspoon brown mustard seeds

2 tomatoes, chopped

3 cups green beans, chopped

Dash of cayenne pepper

Thai basil or cilantro

1 teaspoon tumeric

Salt to taste

Heat the oil in a pot. Add the ginger, cumin seeds and mustard seeds. Sauté over medium heat until the mustard seeds pop, but don't burn. Add the tomatoes and sauté for 2 to 3 minutes, stirring frequently until they become mushy. Stir in the tumeric, green beans, salt and cayenne, and simmer until the beans are tender, about 15 minutes. Adjust salt and add the basil or cilantro. Serve over rice.

SAGE-ROASTED SUMMER SQUASH

Contributed by Wintergreen Farm in Noti, Oregon.

4 medium summer squash

2 Tablespoons olive oil

2 Tablespoons chopped fresh sage

1 Tablespoon minced garlic

Salt and pepper to taste

Preheat the oven to 350°F. Cut the squash on a 1-inch dice. Toss with the other ingredients and roast until tender, about 15 to 20 minutes. Season with salt and pepper to taste.

OIL-ROASTED GREEN BEANS, POTATOES AND FENNEL

2 fennel bulbs

1½ pounds small red potatoes

1½ pounds green beans

⅓ cup olive oil

1 teaspoon coarse salt

Preheat the oven to 425°F. Cut the tops off the fennel, then wash and quarter. Cut the potatoes into fingers. Top and tail the green beans. Toss together the fennel, potatoes and olive oil. Spread on a baking sheet, sprinkle with salt. Bake 30 minutes. Toss in the beans and bake another 10 minutes.

SUMMER BAKED GOODS AND TASTY TREATS

What to have for dessert in the summer? Berries! Lots of berries! And melon—sweet, juicy, dripping-with-sunshine melon. And peaches, just off the tree. For me, summer desserts are all about fruit; most of the time I don't bother cooking it or adding sugar. But there are occasions when a pie or a crisp is called for, or you need some sauce for a bowl of ice cream. Here are a few ideas:

BERRY GOOD SAUCE

6 cups berries of your choice, such as blueberries, blackberries, strawberries, raspberries, or a mixture

½ cup sugar, or more to taste

Rinse the berries and pour them into a wide stainless steel skillet or pot. Sprinkle the sugar over them and cook over medium heat until the berries begin to soften and release their juices (about 2 minutes). Remove from heat, pour into a serving bowl and let sit a few minutes. Spoon over ice cream, or serve in a bowl drizzled with heavy cream, or over biscuits for a quick warm shortcake.

Variations: Use more sugar if you like a sweeter sauce (or if using early berries, which tend to be a bit more tart). A bit of lemon juice or lemon zest is good too. For a special treat, try adding a teaspoon of lavender blossoms. If you prefer a thicker sauce, add 1 teaspoon of cornstarch along with the sugar.

BLACKBERRY COBBLER

1 cup sugar

2 Tablespoons cornstarch

2 Tablespoons quick-cooking tapioca

6 cups blackberries, rinsed

1 teaspoon grated lemon peel

1 Tablespoon lemon juice

2 cups unbleached white flour

1 Tablespoon baking powder

1 teaspoon salt

2 sticks cold butter, cut into chunks

1 cup cream or milk (whipping cream, half-and-half, whole milk, 2%—your choice)

In a large bowl, combine ¾ cups sugar, the cornstarch, tapioca, blackberries, lemon peel and juice. Mix gently, then transfer to a shallow 3- to 4-quart baking dish.

Sift together the flour, baking powder, salt and ¼ cup sugar. With a pastry blender, cut in the butter until coarse crumbs form. Add the cream or milk and stir just until a soft crumbly dough forms.

Divide the dough into ¼ cup portions and flatten each to about ½-inch thick. Arrange evenly over the fruit.

Bake at 350°F, until the topping is golden and the fruit is bubbling, about 45 minutes. Serve warm or at room temperature, with ice cream or fresh cream drizzled over each serving.

FALL · September · October · November

By September it has been hot and dry for so long that the idea of rain ever returning to the valley seems but a pipe dream. The fields are brown, maple leaves have lost their lush green luster, seasonal creeks have dwindled to a few scattered pools. But the evenings are filled with cricket songs and the blackberries are juicy and sweet with the summer sun. In time, of course, the rains do return, softening the earth, washing the dust off the leaves and heralding in the fall.

Autumn is harvest time. Tomatoes are ripening on the vine as fast as you can pick them. They can be dried and soaked in olive oil, or cooked into tomato sauce for pasta dishes in December. Corn is piled high in the market — it can be blanched, scraped off the cob, and frozen for stews and soups. Apples come into their own — what you can't eat fresh can be sliced and frozen into ready-to-go pies. It is time, too, to gather the last of the summer's herbs, some to dry, and some to make into pesto, to be brought out in the middle of winter for a welcome taste of summer.

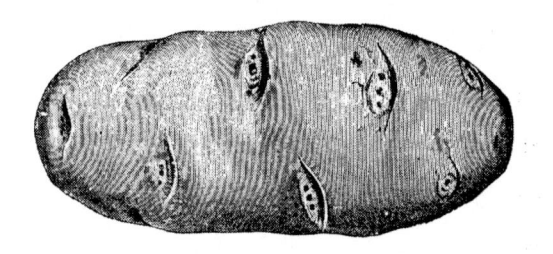

IN SEASON

Early fall (September and sometimes October) can feel like summer. You will still find the bounty of summer available: tomatoes, basil, eggplant, green beans, and so forth. As the days shorten and the nights become cooler—and the first frost hits—these summer flavors will slip away.

Apples	**Hazelnuts**
Beets	**Leeks**
Bok Choi	**Lettuce**
Broccoli	**Melons**
Brussels Sprouts	**Mushrooms**
Burdock Root	**Onions**
Cabbage	**Parsnips**
Carrots	**Pears**
Cauliflower	**Potatoes**
Celeriac	**Pumpkins**
Corn	**Spinach**
Eggplant	**Swiss Chard**
Fennel (bulbing)	**Tomatoes**
Figs	**Turnips**
Garlic	**Walnuts**
Grapes	

SEASON FEATURES

Brussels Sprouts: After the first frost, over-wintering cole crops, like Brussels sprouts, will sweeten up. But if you buy Brussels in the grocery store you may be getting sprouts from California, where they have not had the opportunity to sweeten. Here is another big incentive to buy local! Look for whole stalks of sprouts in your farmers market. To cook them, cut an x into the bottom of the stem on larger sprouts, leave smaller sprouts whole, and steam until just tender. Toss with a bit of butter and lemon juice.

Alternatively, stir-fry by peeling the leaves off the heads, slicing up the core and stir-frying over fairly high heat for a few minutes with some fresh ginger, garlic, red pepper flakes and sesame oil. When the leaves are tender, season with tamari sauce. Or sauté them: Cut the sprouts into quarters, sauté with butter, caraway seeds and onion. Then add a splash of cider vinegar and cook down for a few minutes, until the sprouts are glazed.

Burdock Root: This long slender root vegetable is native to Siberia but content to grow here as well. Scrub it, but don't peel, as most of the nutrients are in the skin. It takes about twice as long to cook as carrots and is wonderful in soups and stews.

Cabbage: Sauté onions, apples, raisins and cabbage in butter for a tasty fall side dish. Grated cabbage is wonderful added to green salad, or in combination with young kale leaves, beet greens and chard leaves. Shred cabbage, carrots, kohlrabi, turnips and toss with your favorite vinaigrette for a non-lettuce based salad.

Fennel Bulb has a light anise taste, with the crunch of celery. Slice the bulb thin and add to salads for an interesting twist. Add to soups, stews or a roasted vegetable medley.

Leeks: Use leeks where you might use an onion but prefer a more delicate flavor, as in soups, omelets, sauces or fillings. Leeks are particularly good in puréed soups, as they melt down into a lovely smooth texture. The green portion of leeks should not be added to puréed soups, however, as it will contribute a muddied color, but all of the green leaves can be used to make vegetable stock.

Mushrooms: In the fall, mushroom hunters, both amateur and professional, head to the hills in droves, returning to favorite haunts to seek out chanterelles, morels, matsutake, black trumpets, fresh hedgehogs and other delicacies native to our area. Fresh and dried mushrooms can be found in farmers markets, some grocery stores, and on the internet. They lend a wonderful earthiness to soups, stews and casseroles. Sauté chopped fresh mushrooms in butter for an exquisite omelette filling, or toss with pasta. Dried mushrooms need only to be soaked in boiling water until soft, roughly chopped and then tossed into a soup of pot. Toss in the soaking water as well!

KINPIRA (SIMMERED BURDOCK ROOT)

I first tasted kinpira when I lived in Japan. I later discovered that burdock can be grown here in the Pacific Northwest. Burdock was traditionally used in China as a medicinal food. In Japan, it has been part of the diet since the tenth century, when it was said to be a source of energy and an aid to recovering from illness. If you cannot find burdock, this recipe is fine with carrots.

1 medium or 2 small burdock roots, scrubbed with a brush, or 3 medium carrots

2 Tablespoons canola oil

2 Tablespoons sake

2 Tablespoons soy sauce

1 scant Tablespoon sugar

¼ teaspoon red pepper flakes (optional)

Cut the burdock or carrot into 2-inch long julienne strips. Place the burdock in water as you go to keep it from discoloring. Heat the oil in a frying pan over medium high heat. Add the burdock and stir-fry for about 3 minutes, until the vegetable starts to soften. Add the sake to the pan, stir in the soy sauce and sugar, and continue to cook over medium heat until the liquid has been almost completely reduced. Stir occasionally to keep the vegetable from sticking to the pan. Flavor with red pepper flakes, if you like. Serve at room temperature. Keeps about a week when refrigerated in a sealed container.

DRIED TOMATO PESTO

Make this in the early fall, when fresh basil is available, or during the winter using frozen basil purée.

1 cup dried tomatoes, reconstituted with water, or drained of oil if oil-packed

½ cup grated Parmesan cheese

¼ cup fresh basil or 1 to 2 cubes basil purée

½ cup walnuts

3 cloves garlic

¼ to ½ cup olive oil

1 Tablespoon balsamic vinegar

½ teaspoon salt

Blend all ingredients in a food processor. Correct the amount of basil, vinegar and salt to your taste.

Spread on crostini or crackers. Add to sandwiches for a nice zing. Or for a main dish, thin the pesto with a bit more olive oil, toss with pasta, and top with grated cheese.

BARTLETT PEAR SALAD WITH ROGUE CREAMERY BLUE CHEESE, TOASTED HAZELNUTS AND MESCLUN GREENS

Contributed by Marché Restaurant in Eugene. A good early fall salad, when the Bartlett pears have just ripened and the first mesclun greens of the season are available.

½ pound mesclun greens

3 ounces hazelnuts

4 ounces Rogue Creamery blue cheese, crumbled

1 large ripe Bartlett pear

VINAIGRETTE

1 teaspoon minced shallot

2 teaspoons sherry vinegar

Pinch salt

3 teaspoons walnut or hazelnut oil

3 teaspoons extra virgin olive oil

Freshly ground black pepper

Make the vinaigrette: Place the shallot, vinegar and salt in a small bowl and allow to marinate for up to an hour. Whisk in the walnut and olive oils until emulsified. Season with freshly ground black pepper.

Wash the greens and dry them well.

Place the hazelnuts on a cookie sheet in a 325°F oven for 3 to 4 minutes. When they are golden and aromatic, remove and allow to cool before chopping coarsely.

Core and slice the pear.

To assemble the salad, toss the mesclun greens with half the vinaigrette. Divide the greens among 4 salad plates, piling them high in the center. Divide the pear slices among the four plates, and sprinkle each with blue cheese and hazelnuts. Drizzle the remaining dressing as needed.

FALL SALADS

KOHLRABI AND SUNGOLD TOMATO SALAD

Contributed by Sweetwater Farm in Creswell, Oregon.

1 or more kohlrabi, peeled

¼ to ½ pint sungold cherry tomatoes

⅓ cup finely grated Parmesan cheese

2 Tablespoons good quality balsamic vinegar

Remove all the fibrous skin from the kohlrabi. Grate the kohlrabi into a mound on a serving plate or individual dishes. Slice the cherry tomatoes in half and place cut side up on top of the kohlrabi. Sprinkle with Parmesan cheese until lightly covered. Drizzle a few splashes of balsamic vinegar over the dish. It is lovely if somewhat unusual looking, and the flavors are great together—a dish which is definitely greater than the sum of its parts.

RAW BEET SALAD

3 cups peeled and grated raw beets (about 3 beets, they can be a combination of red, golden and Chiogga beets)

2 cups peeled and grated raw carrots, or a combination of carrots, parsnips and turnips

1 large apple, grated, but not peeled

½ cup chopped parsley

½ cup toasted pumpkin seeds

Dressing of choice (a tahini-lemon dressing is nice)

Toss the raw vegetables with the dressing. Just before serving, add the pumpkin seeds.

COLESLAW WITH GINGER-MUSTARD DRESSING

1 medium cabbage, either red or green or a combination, shredded

4 carrots, peeled and grated

1 small sweet onion, minced

2 Tablespoons cider vinegar

4 Tablespoons lemon juice

2 Tablespoons Dijon mustard

2 cloves garlic, minced

2 teaspoons grated fresh ginger

1 Tablespoon sugar

⅔ cup olive oil

¼ cup cilantro, minced

Salt and pepper to taste

Toss the cabbage, carrot and onion together in a bowl. Whisk together the vinegar, lemon juice, mustard, garlic, ginger and sugar. Add the oil and cilantro, and season with salt and pepper to taste. Toss with the vegetables and let the flavors become acquainted for 10 minutes before serving.

KOHLRABI AND CARROT SALAD

Adapted from *Kitchen Gardener* magazine.

4 small kohlrabi

2 medium carrots

1 teaspoon salt

8 teaspoons unseasoned rice wine vinegar

2 teaspoons sugar

Pinch ground cayenne pepper

¼ cup fresh mint leaves, or to taste

¼ cup cilantro

½ cup coarsely chopped dry-roasted unsalted peanuts

Peel the carrots and kohlrabi. Cut into ⅛-inch matchsticks. Put in a bowl and sprinkle with about 1 teaspoon salt, tossing thoroughly. Set aside for 10 minutes or so, then squeeze out as much moisture as you can by rolling the vegetables in a clean tea towel and wringing it over the sink. Pat dry. Put the vegetables back in the bowl and add the vinegar, sugar and cayenne. Toss and adjust the seasonings. Tear up or chop the mint and cilantro leaves and add them. Toss well. Garnish with nuts.

BARLEY AND LENTIL SOUP WITH SWISS CHARD

Adapted from *Bon Appétit* magazine.

1 Tablespoon olive oil

1 large onion, chopped

2 carrots, diced

2 stalks celery, diced

4 large cloves garlic, minced

¼ cup minced parsley

2½ teaspoons ground cumin

6 to 10 cups vegetable or chicken stock

⅔ cup pearl barley

4 cups chopped fresh tomatoes or one 28-ounce can tomatoes plus juice

1 cup small green or brown lentils

4 cups packed coarsely chopped Swiss chard (coarse stems removed)

2 Tablespoons dried dill

Heat the oil in a soup pot over medium heat. Add the onions, carrots and celery, and sauté until the onions are golden brown. Add the garlic and parsley, stir another minute. Add the cumin, broth and barley. Bring to a boil and reduce to a simmer for about 25 minutes. Add the tomatoes, with their juices, and the lentils. Cover and simmer until the lentils are tender, about 30 minutes.

Add the chard, cover and simmer until tender. Stir in the dill and season with salt and pepper to taste. If you use red chard, you can finely chop some of the stems and sprinkle them over the top to add some color and crunch.

MINESTRONE

Minestrone is one of our family staples. Each pot is always different, and each pot is always good! There are as many ways to make minestrone as there are cooks making it, so the following is but a guideline, to be altered depending on your mood, the time of year, what is available, and who you are feeding.

5 cups stock (vegetable or chicken, as you wish)

2 stalks celery, minced

3 carrots, minced

1 onion, minced

3 Tablespoons olive oil

2 cloves garlic, minced

1 large potato, chopped

¼ pound green beans, snapped into ½-inch lengths

2 medium zucchini, chopped

½ head cabbage, shredded

8 to 9 fresh plum tomatoes or 1 large can, chopped

1 bay leaf

Good handful chopped parsley

⅓ cup chopped basil

1 can cannellini or kidney beans

Salt and pepper to taste

Red wine vinegar to taste

Heat the olive oil in a soup pot. Sauté the celery, carrots and onion until the onion is soft. Add the garlic and sauté another minute. Add the stock and bay leaf, bring to a boil and reduce to simmer. Add the potato and green beans, simmer a few minutes, until almost tender. Add the cabbage and tomatoes, and then a few minutes later, the zucchini. Add the parsley, basil and beans and cook until the vegetables are done, but not mushy (especially the zucchini). Add salt and pepper to taste.

Adjust seasonings: Maybe you like more basil, some oregano, a splash of red wine vinegar to give it a kick. Use red wine for part of the stock. Play with the ingredients: Add browned sweet Italian sausage (from your local meat market) or sauté some mushrooms and toss them in. Leave out the potato and add some cooked elbow macaroni at the end. If you are making minestrone in late fall or winter, leave out the zucchini and green beans, and use the canned tomatoes. Edamame are good too. Cubes of winter squash make a creamy winter minestrone. Oh, the variations are endless! Whatever you do, pass freshly grated Parmesan to sprinkle on each bowl, and dunk hunks of good chewy bread as you go.

THE REAL DEAL CREAM OF TOMATO SOUP

This is like the soup you might remember from childhood, only not from a can. My kids prefer theirs with grilled cheese sandwiches.

5 Tablespoons butter

½ cup chopped onion

4 Tablespoons flour

2 cups milk

1 bay leaf

1½ teaspoons sugar

1½ teaspoons salt

½ teaspoon baking soda

5 cups chopped tomatoes (fresh tomatoes are sublime, but canned tomatoes are perfectly acceptable for a mid-winter soup)

Melt the butter in a soup pot. Add the onion and cook over medium heat, stirring until softened, but not browned. Sprinkle flour over the onion and continue to stir and cook for a few more minutes. Slowly add the milk, bay leaf, sugar and salt. Continue to cook and stir until slightly thickened.

Stir the baking soda into the tomatoes (this will keep the milk from curdling). Add the tomatoes to the soup pot. Bring just to a simmer and cook until the tomatoes have broken down (longer if using fresh tomatoes). Remove from heat and put through a food mill or strainer to remove the seeds. Taste and correct seasonings. Reheat just before serving. A sprinkle of chopped fresh basil is nice, if you still have some in your garden.

SWISS CHARD WITH CURRANTS AND WALNUTS

Contributed by Hey Bales! Farm in Lorane, Oregon.

⅓ **cup butter**

1 Tablespoon currants

2 Tablespoons golden raisins

1 bunch Swiss chard, stemmed and chopped

1 Tablespoon olive oil

½ **medium red onion, thinly sliced**

Salt and pepper to taste

2 cloves garlic, minced

1 pound penne pasta

⅓ **cup walnuts, chopped and toasted**

Grated Parmesan

Melt the butter over low heat until golden brown. Strain and discard the solids, reserving the golden butter. Cook the penne in a large pot of well-salted water until al dente. Cover the currants and raisins with hot water and drain when plump. Sauté the onion in olive oil for about 5 minutes, then season with salt and pepper. Add the garlic and chard to the onion, then sauté until the chard is tender, about 4 to 5 minutes. Toss the pasta with the browned butter, chard mixture, drained currants and raisins, and nuts. Serve with grated Parmesan cheese.

CALZONE

Contributed by Wintergreen Farm in Noti, Oregon.

DOUGH

1½ teaspoons dry yeast

1 Tablespoon honey

1 cup warm water

1½ teaspoons salt

2½ cups flour

FILLING

1 pound ricotta cheese

2 cloves garlic, crushed

1 pound komatsuna or other greens

2 cups packed grated mozzarella

½ cup minced onion

½ cup grated Parmesan cheese

Dash nutmeg

2 Tablespoons butter

Salt and pepper to taste

Mix together the yeast, honey and water. Add the salt and flour. Knead 10 to 15 minutes. Cover and set in a warm place to rise, until doubled in bulk, about 1 hour. Prepare the filling while the dough is rising.

Wash, stem and finely chop the komatsuna. Steam quickly, on medium high heat, adding no additional water. When wilted and deep green, remove (using a slotted spoon) to a mixing bowl. Sauté the onion and garlic in butter until translucent and soft. Combine all ingredients, mix well, add salt and pepper to taste. Set aside.

Punch down the dough. Divide into 6 sections. Roll out each into a ¼-inch thick round.

Fill each round with ½ to ¾ cup filling, placing filling on one half of the circle, leaving a ½-inch rim. Moisten the rim with water, fold the empty side over the filling, and crimp the edge with a fork. Prick here and there. Bake on an oiled tray in a preheated 450°F oven for 15 to 20 minutes, until crisp and lightly browned. Brush each calzone with a little butter as it emerges from the oven.

Note: This is a good spring recipe as well. You could substitute other greens for the komatsuna, or use a combination of greens.

POTATO AND CHARD BAKE

1 pound thin-skinned potatoes

1 Tablespoon olive oil

1 very large bunch Swiss chard, stems removed and leaves cut into ½-inch strips

3 cloves garlic, minced

4 ounces goat cheese or feta cheese

1 cup milk

3 large eggs

½ teaspoon salt

Put the potatoes in a pot of water and boil until just tender. Cool and cut into ½-inch slices. In a large pan, heat the oil and cook the chard until just wilted, stirring often. Add the garlic and sauté another minute or two. Remove from heat and season to taste with salt and pepper. Oil a 9 x 9 inch pan and spread the potato slices over the bottom. Top with the chard and sprinkle with the cheese. Whisk together the milk, eggs and salt, and pour over the potatoes and chard. Cover with foil and bake 45 to 50 minutes in a 350°F oven, until set. Cool 5 to 10 minutes before you cut and serve.

WHITE BEAN, SQUASH, KALE AND OLIVE STEW

Contributed by Wintergreen Farm in Noti, Oregon.

¼ **cup olive oil**

3 large onions, chopped

6 cloves garlic, minced

3½ pounds winter squash, peeled, seeded and cut into 1½ inch pieces

1½ cups vegetable broth

1 cup Kalamata olives, pitted and halved

3 red bell peppers, seeded and cut into 1½ inch pieces

1 large bunch kale, thick stems removed and leaves cut cross-wise into 2-inch strips

1 Tablespoon dried sage

Two 15-ounce cans cannellini beans, drained and rinsed

Freshly grated Romano cheese

Heat the oil in a Dutch oven over medium heat. Add the onions and garlic, and sauté until tender, about 10 minutes. Add the squash, sauté further. Add the bell peppers and stir to coat with the onion mix. Add the broth. Cover and simmer until the squash is tender, about 10 minutes. Mix the kale and sage into the stew. Cover and cook until the kale wilts, stirring occasionally, about 8 minutes. Add the beans and olives and stir until heated through. Season to taste with salt and pepper. Transfer the stew to a large shallow bowl. Sprinkle generously with cheese.

SALLY'S FAVORITE SAUSAGE AND PEPPERS

Contributed by Sweetwater Farm in Creswell, Oregon. Sally is one of their CSA members.

1 Italian sausage

2 cloves garlic, sliced

2 pieces Italian bread or baguette

1 medium or 2 small bell peppers, cut into thin strips

1 medium tomato, chopped

½ onion, chopped

1 sprig rosemary

Salt and red chili pepper flakes to taste

Parmesan cheese

Put the sausage in the freezer for 10 minutes to make it easier to handle and hold together better while cooking. Slice and brown the sausage. Set aside. Add the onions, garlic, peppers and rosemary to the pan and sauté until the peppers are limp. Add the tomato and sausage. Cook until the sausage is cooked through. Remove the rosemary. Add salt and red chili pepper flakes to taste. Serve on bread with a dusting of Parmesan.

CHARD AND POTATO ENCHILADAS

1 pound Swiss chard, ribs removed and leaves cut into ribbons

1 Tablespoon olive oil

1 medium onion, chopped

3 cloves garlic, minced

½ teaspoon salt

2 large or 3 small potatoes, cooked and cubed

1 to 2 cups shredded jack or cheddar cheese

12 corn tortillas

Home-Made Enchilada Sauce

In a large frying pan, heat the oil and sauté the onion over medium-low heat, until it begins to turn golden. Add the garlic and cook another minute. Then add the greens in batches, cooking until they are just tender. Season with salt, then stir in the potatoes.

Lightly oil a 13 x 9 inch baking dish. Spread ½ cup enchilada sauce over the bottom. Heat each tortilla briefly on a hot cast-iron griddle (no need to grease it) or over a flame, until the tortilla is pliable. Dip the tortilla into the enchilada sauce to coat each side. Spoon about ¼ cup of the greens onto the middle of the tortilla. Top with grated cheese, roll up and place in the pan. This is kind of messy work; it is helpful to have one person warming the tortillas at the stove, and another dipping and filling at the counter.

Tuck the enchiladas pretty close together. Top with a bit more enchilada sauce (not too much, as you don't want the enchiladas swimming in sauce) and a bit more grated cheese. Cover and bake 35 minutes at 350°F, until the sauce bubbles and the cheese melts. Serve hot, with sour cream if desired, more sauce if you like things wet, and if available, a bowl of chopped fresh cilantro.

Variations: In the winter, make enchiladas with kale. If you can find them, try the traditional Mexican greens called *quelites* (lamb's quarters). If you don't feel like making enchiladas, just pass warm tortillas, a bowl of greens, and Mexican *queso fresco, cotilla* cheese, or grated Parmesan (instead of cheddar or jack cheese) and make soft tacos at the table.

HOME-MADE ENCHILADA SAUCE

3 Tablespoons canola oil

1 Tablespoon flour

¼ cup chili powder

2 cups chicken stock or vegetable stock

10 ounces tomato paste

1 teaspoon dried oregano

1 teaspoon ground cumin

½ teaspoon salt

In a saucepan, heat the oil and stir in the flour. Cook for 1 minute. Add the chili powder and cook another minute. Add the stock, tomato paste, oregano and cumin. Stir to combine. Bring to a boil, reduce to low and simmer for 15 minutes. The sauce will thicken as it simmers. Taste and add more spices as desired. Makes 2½ cups sauce, which can be frozen. If you buy the chili powder in the bulk section, you might be able to choose from several degrees of heat. Pick what works for you. This is easy to make and so much more flavorful than canned enchilada sauce.

TEMPATO PATTIES

Adapted from a *Vegetarian Times* recipe. We enjoy these with a salad for a light supper, but they are also fine with fried eggs at breakfast.

2 to 3 thin-skinned potatoes (red, Yukon gold, etc., or an equal amount of fingerlings), chopped into ¼-inch cubes

1 onion, finely chopped

2 to 3 cups chopped greens, such as kale, chard, spinach, or a mixture

1 Tablespoon olive oil, plus more to brush on the patties

8 ounces tempeh (Surata produces tempeh locally)

1 large egg, beaten

⅓ cup flour

¼ cup minced chives

2 Tablespoons soy sauce

1 Tablespoon chopped rosemary

2 cloves garlic, minced

½ teaspoon minced fresh thyme

½ teaspoon minced fresh sage

½ teaspoon minced fresh oregano

Steam the tempeh for 20 minutes, cool slightly and pulse in a food processor (the steaming makes it break up more easily). Steam or boil the potatoes until soft. In a large frying pan, heat the olive oil over medium heat, and cook the onion until soft. Add the greens and cook until just tender. Stir the tempeh, potatoes, onions, greens and the remaining ingredients together in a large bowl. I use my hands to knead it together. Form 2-inch balls, flatten and place them on a lightly greased baking pan. Brush the patties with olive oil and bake at 450°F for 10 minutes. Flip the patties over, brush with olive oil and bake another 10 minutes, until brown and crispy.

CRANBERRY SAUCE FOR GRILLED OR POACHED SALMON

Contributed by Lynne Fessenden, executive director of the Willamette Valley Farm & Food Coalition.

3 cups cranberries

½ cup water or apple juice

½ cup honey or sugar

2 shallots, finely chopped

2 Tablespoons olive oil or butter

½ cup dry white wine

1 Tablespoon Dijon mustard

Rinse the cranberries and boil them in the water or juice over low heat until soft and thick. Add the honey or sugar and adjust as preferred. Set aside. Sauté the shallots in the olive oil until soft. Stir in the wine and mustard. Simmer slowly until reduced. Stir in the cranberry sauce. Salt to taste. Serve warm, or at room temperature, over grilled or poached salmon.

FALL MAIN DISHES

BLACKBERRY SAUCE FOR SALMON

Contributed by Lynne Fessenden. Lynne uses buttermilk, which gives a nice tang to sweet late summer berries. Earlier berries are more tart, so the half-and-half might suit them better.

4 cups blackberries

4 to 6 shallots, chopped

2 Tablespoons olive oil or butter

½ cup buttermilk or half-and-half

Blend the berries in a food processor, then put them through a sieve to remove the seeds. Sauté the shallots in olive oil until soft. Blend the shallots and berry paste in the food processor. Pour sauce back into sauté pan, stir in buttermilk or half-and-half. Cook over low heat until reduced. Salt to taste.

PEDER'S FAVORITE SALMON MARINADE

Contributed by Lynne Fessenden.

¼ cup olive oil

¼ cup teriyaki sauce

¼ cup Dijon mustard

3 Tablespoons prepared horseradish

2 Tablespoons brown sugar

1 teaspoon rice vinegar

Whisk all ingredients together in a small bowl. Set aside ⅓ of the marinade. Pour the rest into a zip-top bag with 4 to 6 pounds of salmon fillets. Marinate for 15 to 30 minutes. Remove the salmon, scraping off the sauce to use as a baste while grilling. Grill the fish. Serve with the reserved sauce.

FALL STEW

1 cup pinto beans, soaked and cooked until tender, or 1 can drained

1 can hominy

1 pound fresh tomatoes

1 Tablespoon chopped fresh oregano

1 Tablespoon ground cumin

½ teaspoon ground cloves

1 Tablespoon canola oil

1 onion, minced

3 cloves garlic, minced

1 Tablespoon paprika

3 cups winter squash, cubed

3 potatoes, cubed

2 carrots, chopped

2 to 3 cups vegetable, chicken or mushroom broth

1 chipotle chile

2 roasted Anaheim chiles, chopped

In a kettle, heat the oil and sauté the onion until soft. Add the garlic and spices and sauté a few minutes more. Add 1 cup broth and the tomatoes. Cook down a bit. Add the rest of the broth and the squash and cook until almost tender. Add the carrots and potatoes, Anaheim and chipotle chiles, beans and hominy. Cook until quite tender. Remove the chipotle when the stew is spicy enough for your taste. Serve with sour cream, if desired, and fresh cilantro, if available.

RATATOUILLE WITH POLENTA

Ratatouille is a vegetable stew (with a fancy name), and, as with all stews, it is quite adaptable to your tastes and the seasons.

¼ cup olive oil

1 medium onion, chopped

2 sweet peppers, chopped

1 to 2 zucchini or summer squash, cut into 1-inch cubes

1 small eggplant, peeled and cut into 1-inch cubes

4 to 5 cloves garlic, minced

2 large tomatoes, quartered

1 bay leaf

1 teaspoon oregano

1 Tablespoon chopped basil

1 sprig fresh rosemary

¼ cup dry red wine

½ cup tomato juice

2 Tablespoons tomato paste

Salt and pepper to taste

¼ cup chopped fresh parsley

Grated Parmesan cheese

Heat the olive oil in a large heavy soup pot or Dutch oven. Add the onion, garlic and bay leaf. Sauté over medium heat, until the onion softens but is not brown. Add the eggplant, wine, tomato juice and herbs. Stir to mix well, then cover and simmer for 10 to 15 minutes. When the eggplant can be easily pricked with a fork, add the zucchini and peppers. Simmer another 10 minutes.

Add the tomatoes and tomato paste, and salt and pepper to taste. Mix well and continue to cook until all the vegetables are quite tender. Stir in the parsley. Adjust seasonings, adding more salt, pepper, or maybe more garlic or basil. Remove the bay leaf and rosemary, and serve over Polenta. Top with grated Parmesan.

POLENTA

7 cups cold water

1 Tablespoon salt

2 cups polenta (coarse yellow cornmeal)

Combine the water and salt in a deep pan over medium heat. Pour in the cornmeal, stirring constantly in one direction with a whisk or wooden spoon. This prevents lumps from forming and keeps the boiling temperature constant, which results in a soft creamy polenta. Stir until the polenta begins to pull away from the sides of the pan, about 30 minutes. Employ children or spouse to assist with stirring.

Pour the polenta into a serving dish and top with a generous pat of butter or grated Parmesan cheese. For a creamier polenta, substitute milk for the water, and stir in crumbled goat cheese or smoked cheese or grated cheddar cheese at the end of the cooking time.

POLENTA WITH GREENS

Polenta (use the recipe on page 167)

1 pound kale or chard or a combination, cut into ½-inch ribbons

4 ounces fresh mushrooms, such as button, shiitake, chanterelle, etc.

4 Tablespoons olive oil

1 clove garlic, minced, or more to taste

½ cup chicken or vegetable stock

1 Tablespoon chopped fresh thyme

1 Tablespoon lemon zest

⅔ cup grated Parmesan cheese

In a large skillet, sauté the mushrooms in 2 tablespoons of the oil until tender. Add the greens (you may need to add them in batches until they wilt). Add the garlic and broth. Simmer until the broth reduces a bit. Stir in the thyme, lemon peel and 2 more tablespoons of oil. Season to taste with salt and pepper.

Pour the polenta into a large platter or serving dish and top with the greens. Serve with Parmesan cheese.

Variations: Fry some bacon or pancetta first, remove from the pan while you sauté the mushrooms, then add it back with the greens. Or try omitting the thyme and lemon zest, adding ½ cup dried tomatoes, and then sprinkling some toasted pine nuts on top.

SESAME SOY BRAISED BOK CHOI

Contributed by Wintergreen Farm in Noti, Oregon. Bok choi spans several seasons. You can find it in late spring and again in early fall.

1 head bok choi

2 Tablespoons peanut oil

1 Tablespoon grated fresh ginger

1 Tablespoon minced garlic

1 Tablespoon toasted sesame oil

2 Tablespoons soy sauce

2 teaspoons rice vinegar

1 teaspoon sugar

Salt and pepper to taste

2 Tablespoons sesame seeds

½ cup chicken or vegetable stock

Slice the bok choi leaves and stems into thin ribbons, keeping them separate from each other. Heat the peanut oil in a large pan. Add the stems and stir-fry for 5 minutes. Add the ginger and garlic and fry for a few moments. Add the leaves, stock, sesame oil, soy sauce, vinegar and sugar. Cover and reduce the heat. Simmer for 5 to 8 minutes. Remove the cover and sprinkle with sesame seeds. Increase the heat and cook 2 to 3 minutes, until the excess liquid evaporates. Season with salt and pepper to taste.

SQUASH PANCAKES

Contributed by Wintergreen Farm in Noti, Oregon.

1 egg

1 cup winter squash, cooked and mashed

½ cup flour

1½ to 2 teaspoons sugar

¼ teaspoon salt

½ teaspoon baking powder

¼ teaspoon cinnamon

¼ teaspoon nutmeg

1 teaspoon melted butter

1 Tablespoon milk

Beat the egg and mix it with the squash in a large bowl. In another bowl, sift together the flour, sugar, salt, baking powder and spices. Add the dry ingredients to the squash and egg. Stir in the butter and milk. Mix well and ladle onto a heated griddle. Cook on one side until bubbles appear. Turn and cook on the other side. Makes 6 to 8 pancakes.

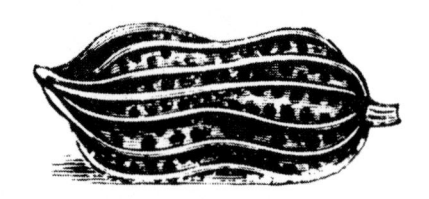

FRIED GREEN TOMATOES

Contributed by Wintergreen Farm in Noti, Oregon.

4 green tomatoes

2 cups buttermilk

1 Tablespoon Tabasco sauce

1 cup yellow cornmeal

1 cup flour

½ teaspoon baking soda

1 teaspoon salt

1 teaspoon pepper

½ cup peanut oil

4 Tablespoons unsalted butter

Core the top of each tomato and cut into ½-inch thick slices. Mix the buttermilk and Tabasco together in a pan. Place the tomato slices in the buttermilk mix and marinate 1 hour, turning occasionally.

In a shallow bowl, combine the cornmeal, flour, baking soda, salt and pepper. Drain the tomato slices and dredge carefully in the breading mix. Place the slices on a baking sheet and refrigerate 30 minutes to allow breading to dry.

In a heavy 12-inch skillet, heat the oil over medium heat. Add the butter. When hot, carefully place as many tomato slices in the skillet as will fit loosely in a single layer. Don't crowd them or the fat temperature will drop and the tomatoes will be greasy. Pan fry 45 seconds to 1 minute on each side, until a nice golden brown. Remove to a plate lined with paper towels. Hold in a 200°F oven until all the tomatoes are cooked.

ROAST ROOTS

Combining root vegetables in a roasting pan is one of our favorite fall and winter treats. We vary the assortment of vegetables according to what is available. Some ideas are listed below. Experiment and find your favorite combo!

2 parsnips

3 carrots

4 potatoes

1 fennel bulb, 1 small celery root, or 1 sweet onion (optional)

Peel the parsnips and carrots and cut into 1-inch pieces. Scrub, but don't peel, the potatoes, then cut them into fingers. If using the fennel bulb or celery root, remove the tough or brown layers, cut in half lengthwise, and then into ¼-inch chips. If you don't have fennel or celery root, you might substitute a sweet onion. Toss all the vegetables with olive oil, sprinkle with salt and pepper, and spread in a single layer on a baking sheet. Roast at 450°F for 20 minutes. Then turn them over and roast another 10 minutes or so, until the roots are tender inside and crisp outside. If desired, sprinkle with balsamic vinegar before serving.

Variations: Add some peeled garlic cloves (they are roots too!). Turnips and rutabagas are also nice additions. Kohlrabi doesn't mind being roasted. Chunks of winter squash can be added—peel the thick-skinned ones like butternut, but you can seed and slice up delicata squash and roast it with the skin on. Or mix some fresh herbs, like rosemary and/or thyme, into the olive oil.

If you have leftover roast roots, you can toss them with some dressing to make a salad. Or make a soup, either puréed or chunky.

SQUISHED SQUASH

Adapted from Bon Appétit magazine, and so named by my kids, who request it for Thanksgiving each year.

2 large butternut squash, cut in half lengthwise and seeded

½ stick butter

2 Tablespoons frozen orange juice concentrate

2 Tablespoons honey

2 Tablespoons grated fresh ginger

1 teaspoon grated orange peel

1 teaspoon grated lemon peel

¾ teaspoon cinnamon

½ teaspoon allspice, or you can substitute nutmeg

Place the squash cut side down on a lightly greased baking sheet and bake at 350°F, until very tender when pierced with a fork, about 45 to 50 minutes. (If you are in a time crunch, you can peel the squash, cut it into chunks and steam until very tender.) Let the squash cool until you can handle it, then scoop the flesh out and purée it in a food processor. Transfer to a bowl.

Combine the butter, orange juice concentrate, honey, ginger and orange peel (but not the lemon peel!) in a small heavy saucepan. Boil until the mixture is reduced to ⅓ cup, about 3 minutes. Stir the syrup into the puréed squash. Mix in the lemon peel, cinnamon and allspice or nutmeg. Season with salt and pepper to taste. Yum!

STUFFED SQUASH

¼ cup pine nuts, or chopped hazelnuts or walnuts

3 to 4 squash, such as delicata or acorn

2 teaspoons olive oil

1 onion, chopped

4 cloves garlic, minced

1 carrot, finely chopped

1 parsnip, finely chopped

1 teaspoon minced rosemary

1 teaspoon minced thyme

Freshly ground pepper to taste

1 cup uncooked brown rice

½ teaspoon salt

2¼ cups vegetable or chicken stock, or water

½ cup minced parsley

1 large egg, beaten

3 teaspoons fine bread crumbs

Toast the nuts in a toaster oven at 300°F, or in a small cast-iron pan, until fragrant. This doesn't take long, so watch them carefully!

Halve the squash lengthwise and scoop out the seeds. Place the squash, cut side down, on a lightly greased pan. Bake at 350°F, until tender and easily pierced by a fork — about 45 minutes.

While the squash are cooking, heat the oil over medium heat in a skillet with a tight-fitting lid. Add the onion and sauté a few minutes until translucent. Add the garlic, carrot and parsnip. Sauté a few more minutes, then add the herbs, pepper and rice. Sauté another few minutes, stirring often, until the rice is lightly toasted.

Add the salt and stock or water. Stir the mixture, bring it to a boil, then reduce the heat to low and cover. Cook 40 minutes, until all the moisture is absorbed. Remove from heat, keeping the cover on to let the rice rest for 10 minutes.

Stir in the parsley and pine nuts. Season with salt and pepper to taste. Thoroughly mix in the egg.

Preheat the oven to 400°F. Stuff the squash with the rice mixture, pressing down to compact it and rounding it well over the top. Arrange the squash in a large lightly-greased baking dish and sprinkle bread crumbs over the top. Cover tightly with a lid or aluminum foil and bake for 30 minutes. Uncover and bake another 5 to 10 minutes, until the bread crumbs are crispy.

LEMON-GARLIC BROCCOLI

Adapted from *The Cook's Garden*, Shepherd and Ellen Ogden.

1 lemon

3 cloves garlic, minced or pressed

1 Tablespoon toasted sesame oil

¼ cup olive oil

1 large head of broccoli

With a vegetable peeler or lemon zester remove most of the lemon rind in very thin strips. Finely mince the rind. Squeeze the juice from the lemon, and combine the juice, rind, garlic, sesame oil and olive oil in a medium-size bowl. Whisk together until well blended.

Cut the broccoli flowers into small florets. Peel the stalk and cut into 1-inch chunks. Steam until just tender, about 5 minutes. Transfer to a serving dish and toss gently with the lemon-garlic sauce.

HAZELNUT BUTTERMILK PANCAKES WITH BLACKBERRY BUTTER

Adapted from *Dungeness Crabs and Blackberry Cobblers*, Janie Hibler. Rather like having dessert for breakfast! The batter needs to be started the night before.

1 package active dry yeast

½ cup warm water

2½ cups buttermilk, plus extra for thinning

3 eggs

2 cups unbleached white flour, or substitute all or part whole wheat

3 Tablespoons sugar

1 Tablespoon baking soda

1 teaspoon salt

¼ cup finely ground toasted hazelnuts

Blackberry Butter

In a large bowl, dissolve the yeast and a pinch of sugar in warm (105°F) water. Stir in the buttermilk and eggs. Sift together the flour, sugar, baking soda and salt. Add to the wet ingredients and mix well. Cover and place in the refrigerator overnight. In the morning, add a bit more buttermilk if the batter is too thick to easily pour onto the griddle.

Heat a lightly greased griddle and cook the pancakes over medium heat until bubbles rise to the surface and pop. Turn and cook on the other side. Serve with warm Blackberry Butter.

GINGER BAKED APPLES

Adapted from *Kitchen of Light*, Andreas Viestad.

4 large apples

¼ cup local honey

2 Tablespoons minced fresh or candied ginger

2 Tablespoons butter

Remove a one-inch diameter core from each apple (without cutting all the way through to the bottom). In a small bowl, mix the honey and ginger. If the honey has crystallized, heat it briefly in the microwave. Place the apples in a baking dish and fill the cavities with the honey and ginger. Top each with a pat of butter.

Bake at 400°F for 45 minutes, until quite tender. Serve hot or warm, topped with yogurt, sour cream or ice cream as desired.

BLACKBERRY BUTTER

½ cup butter

2 cups fresh blackberries or 1 pound frozen and thawed berries

1 cup sugar

In a medium-size saucepan over low heat, melt the butter and stir in the blackberries and sugar. Cook, stirring, until the sugar is dissolved and the berries have released their juices. You might want to add more sugar, depending on the sweetness of the berries. Serve immediately or store in the refrigerator for up to 2 weeks. Also good on French toast and waffles.

Variations: If you prefer, put the blackberries through a food mill to remove the seeds. Try substituting strawberries or raspberries for all or part of the recipe.

FRESH PEAR/APPLE CRUMBLE PIE

Contributed by River Bend Farm and Pleasant Hill Orchard, in Pleasant Hill, Oregon.

½ cup sugar

2 Tablespoons flour

1 teaspoon grated lemon peel

5 cups sliced pears and apples (approximately 2½ pounds)

3 Tablespoons lemon juice

1 single pie crust

CRUMBLE CRUST TOPPING

½ cup flour

½ cup sugar

½ teaspoon ground ginger

½ teaspoon cinnamon

¼ cup butter

In a large bowl, sprinkle the pears and apples with the lemon juice and peel. Add the flour and sugar and toss to coat the fruit. Mound into the pie crust. Combine the crumble crust ingredients and sprinkle over the fruit. Cover the edges of the crust with foil. Bake at 375°F for 25 minutes. Remove the crust protector and bake another 25 minutes.

PEAR CRISP

1 cup rolled oats

½ cup unbleached white flour

⅔ cup finely chopped walnuts

½ cup brown sugar

½ teaspoon ground cinnamon

½ teaspoon ground ginger

¼ teaspoon ground nutmeg

⅛ teaspoon salt

½ cup cold butter, cut into chunks

4 to 6 cups fresh pear slices, cores removed, but not necessarily peeled

Lemon juice to toss with the pears while you process them

In a large bowl, mix the oats, flour, walnuts, brown sugar, spices and salt. With a pastry cutter, cut the butter into the oat mixture until coarse crumbs form.

Place the pear slices in a shallow 2- to 3-quart baking dish and sprinkle the crumb topping over them. Bake at 350°F, until the topping is golden brown and the fruit is bubbling, about 45 minutes. Serve warm or at room temperature. Lovely with ice cream, or regular cream, or soy milk.

APPLE PIE WITH SAGE

It might sound a bit odd, but the savory character of the sage leaves is well balanced by the tart apples and the sweet spices and sugar.

BUTTER PIE CRUST

1 cup cold unsalted butter

2 cups unbleached flour

Scant ¼ cup sugar

¼ teaspoon salt

¼ cup cold water

2 teaspoons lemon juice

APPLE FILLING

2 to 3 pounds Gravenstein apples, or other juicy tart apples of your choice

Juice of one large lemon

1 cup sugar

2 Tablespoons finely minced sage leaves

2½ Tablespoons flour

¾ teaspoon ground mace or nutmeg

1½ teaspoons cinnamon

¼ teaspoon ground ginger

¼ teaspoon salt

Cut the butter into ½-inch cubes. Mix the flour, sugar and salt in a bowl and cut in the butter until the dough is crumbly and the butter pieces are no bigger than a pea. Try to keep the butter cold as you work; if necessary, place the bowl in the refrigerator to firm up the dough. Sprinkle the cold water evenly over the dough and work it with a fork until the mixture pulls together in a shaggy mess.

Cut the dough in half and pat each piece into a thick flat disk. On a floured work surface, roll out one of the disks to about 12 inches in diameter. Fold in half and transfer gently to a deep dish pie pan. Unfold and ease the dough into the bottom of the pan without stretching it. Cover with plastic wrap and chill.

Roll out the remaining half of the dough as above, then place it on a plate and refrigerate — this will be your top crust.

While the dough chills, make the filling:

Core the apples and cut them into ¼-inch slices, peeled if desired. As you go, toss the apple slices with lemon juice in a large bowl. Sprinkle the sugar and sage over the apples, and toss again to mix. Let stand 10 minutes to let the sugar dissolve. Sprinkle on the flour, spices and salt. Mix well.

Place a heavy rimmed baking sheet on a rack in the lower third of the oven. Preheat the oven to 450°F.

Pile the apples into the pie dish, taking care not to tear the dough and making a mound in the center. Trim the excess dough to ¼ inch past the edge of the dish. Moisten the edge with cold water or the sugary juices left in the bowl. Cover with the top crust. Press with a fork or your fingers to seal and crimp the edges. Cut 6 to 8 vents in the top to let steam escape. If you are feeling extra fancy, cut some of the dough trimmings into leaf shapes, lightly brush the surface of the crust with water, and press the decorations gently onto the top crust.

Rest a sheet of foil on the pie and bake for 20 minutes at 450°F. Reduce the oven to 375°F, remove the foil, and bake another 40 minutes, until the apples inside are tender and the crust is golden. Cover the rim with strips of foil if it is getting too dark. Dust the crust with cinnamon and sugar. Let the pie cool at least an hour, preferably longer. Serve with ice cream or sharp cheddar cheese, if desired.

DISHES TO FIT ANY SEASON

There are quite a few dishes that can be made to suit any season. Soup and salad are two that come easily to mind. Pasta is also hugely adaptable—toss cooked pasta with whatever fresh vegetable is in season, a bit of meat or beans, fresh or frozen herbs, and top with cheese. Frittatas are another good venue for seasonal cooking. Employ what vegetables are available—either steamed or sautéed in the frittata pan—and add bits of cooked potatoes, ends of cheese, and bits of ham. Use the recipe on page 100 as a springboard.

Another dish we make all year long is pizza. Pre-made pizza dough from local bakeries can be purchased easily, but I enjoy making the dough myself on the weekends. Like soups, salads and pasta, pizza presents a sort of culinary blank canvas on which you can compose a myriad of taste combinations. Following are a few ideas.

PIZZA CRUST

Makes one large 15- to 16-inch pizza or two smaller pizzas.

1 package active dry yeast

1 cup plus 2 Tablespoons warm water (105°F)

Pinch of sugar

1 teaspoon salt

4½ Tablespoons olive oil

¾ cup whole wheat flour

2½ cups unbleached white flour

Stir the yeast, water and sugar together and let sit 5 minutes, until foamy. Stir in the oil and salt, then add the flour 1 cup at a time. Mix until all the lumps are gone. Knead 8 to 10 minutes, until the dough is satiny and elastic. Place the dough in an oiled bowl, turn to coat, and cover tightly with plastic wrap. Let rise for 45 minutes to an hour, until doubled.

Roll or lightly press the dough into a flattened ball. Pick it up and stretch it with your fists, from underneath, until it is stretched to about ½- to ¼-inch thin. Place it on a pizza peel that has been sprinkled with cornmeal. Cover with a kitchen towel and let rest about 30 minutes.

While the dough rests, preheat the oven (and pizza stone) to 450°F. Prepare your toppings. When the dough has rested and the oven is up to temperature, add your toppings and slide the composed pizza onto the hot pizza stone.

If you are not using a pizza peel and pizza stone, place the stretched dough on a cookie sheet to rest, then add the toppings and bake as above.

THE KID'S FAVORITE PIZZA

½ cup Roasted Tomato Sauce or other pizza sauce

½ cup grated mozzarella cheese or a mix of mozzarella, Parmesan and fontina

Sliced olives

2 to 3 cloves garlic, minced

Olive oil

Brush olive oil over the entire surface of the pizza dough. With a spoon, spread on the pizza sauce. Sprinkle with olives and minced garlic. Bake for 5 minutes. Add the cheese and bake another 5 minutes.

PESTO PIZZA

½ cup pesto

1 cup steamed broccoli, cut into small pieces

½ cup chopped sun-dried tomatoes

½ cup crumbled feta cheese or goat cheese

Olive oil

Brush some olive oil on the pizza dough, then smear the pesto over the whole thing. Sprinkle with broccoli. Bake for 5 minutes, then add the cheese and sun-dried tomatoes and bake another 5 minutes.

ZUCCHINI AND BASIL PIZZA

½ cup Roasted Tomato Sauce or other pizza sauce

½ cup grated mozzarella cheese or a mix of mozzarella, Parmesan and fontina

1 small zucchini, thinly sliced

¼ cup fresh basil, cut into ribbons

Olive oil

Brush olive oil over the entire surface of the pizza dough. Spread the pizza sauce over the dough. Arrange the zucchini slices. Bake for 5 minutes. Add the cheese and bake another 5 minutes. Top with fresh basil.

PESTO AND FRESH TOMATO PIZZA

½ cup pesto

1 to 2 fresh tomatoes, sliced

½ cup crumbled feta cheese or goat cheese, or grated Parmesan

Olive oil

Brush some olive oil on the pizza dough, then spread on the pesto. Arrange the tomato slices on top of the pesto. Bake for 5 minutes. Add the cheese and bake another 5 minutes.

PIZZA WITH GREENS

1 very large bunch kale, chard, spinach or a mixture, tough stems removed and leaves shredded

2 to 3 cloves garlic, minced

½ cup feta cheese, goat cheese or Parmesan cheese

Olive oil

In a large skillet, heat 2 tablespoons olive oil and add the garlic. Sauté for a minute, until the garlic is fragrant. Add the greens in batches, until tender (spinach and chard won't take as long to cook as kale). Brush the pizza dough with olive oil, top with the greens, and bake for 5 minutes. Add the cheese and bake another 5 minutes.

Let those December winds bellow and blow,
I'm as warm as a July tomato.
Peaches on the shelf,
Potatoes in the bin.
Supper's ready, everybody come on in.
Taste a little of the summer.
Taste a little of the summer.
You can taste a little of the summer—
My grandma's put it all in jars.

— Greg Brown, "Canned Goods"

PUTTING FOOD BY

Putting food by involves one of several methods: canning, drying, freezing or cold storage. If you haven't done it before, canning can be a little intimidating. Drying is certainly less intimidating than canning, but it does require an electric or solar dehydrator. Freezing is by far the simplest method of putting food by. If you don't own a large freezer, perhaps you have a friend or neighbor willing to loan you an unused corner of theirs. Cold storage is great for some vegetables and apples, especially if you have an unused room or basement that is cool and dark.

Check out some books, such as the classic *Putting Food By* by Ruth Hertzberg, Beatrice Vaughan and Janet Greene, and team up with a friend. Processing food in large quantities is much more fun when done in community.

FROZEN BERRIES

Wash and drip dry the berries. De-stem strawberries by poking a large sturdy drinking straw through the bottom of the berry and out through the top — the stem and core will pop right out. Spread the berries on cookie sheets and carefully place them in the freezer. After they are frozen scoop into zip-top bags or freezer containers. Frozen blueberries are good straight from the freezer as a snack — you don't even have to defrost them. Blackberries, raspberries and strawberries are good cooked down into a sauce, or use them in baking. Or blend them with yogurt for a smoothie.

DRIED STRAWBERRIES

Wash the berries and remove the stems and caps. Slice into quarters or thirds and dry on screens set over cookie sheets (for air circulation) in an oven set at 90–140°F. Or place in an electric food dehydrator. Either way, dry until they are somewhat pliable, then store in a cool dry location for up to 6 months, or in the freezer for up to a year.

What to do with dried strawberries? Toss them in granola, in trail mix, into muffin or pancake batter. Or bring some butter to room temperature and blend it with strawberries (about ¼ cup berries to one stick of butter). Let your berry butter rest a day before you slather it on toast or muffins.

FROZEN CORN

Blanch whole cobs of corn for a few minutes and then cut the kernels off the cob. Spread on a cookie sheet and freeze. Store in zip-top bags or freezer containers.

FROZEN TOMATOES

Frozen tomatoes have to be one of the easiest ways to preserve your harvest: when you are besieged with them in September, simply pop whole clean tomatoes into a freezer bag and freeze. In the depths of winter, retrieve them as needed, run them under hot water until their skins slip off, and Bob's your uncle!

DRIED TOMATOES

Any tomato can be dried, but traditionally, the Roma or paste tomatoes are used because they have less juice to evaporate. Here is my process:

Wash the tomatoes. Cut large paste tomatoes in quarters, smaller ones in half, and scoop the seeds out with your finger. (I scoop them into a strainer set over a small bowl, as the resulting tomato juice is intensely flavorful.) Put the tomatoes cut side up on a food dehydrator tray and dry at 130°F. I usually dry them in large batches, starting in the afternoon, letting them dry overnight, and begin taking them off the tray as they appear ready in the morning. They should be leathery and not sticky. I keep dried tomatoes in the freezer in zip-top bags or plastic freezer containers.

You can also dry tomatoes past the leathery stage, until they are a bit crispy, and then grind them into a powder, known in our house as Essence of Summer. Sprinkle the tomato powder on salads, pasta, soup — anywhere you would sprinkle grated cheese.

Cherry tomatoes can be dried easily too. Just cut them in half and squeeze out the seeds. They will dry faster and be more like tomato chips — we eat them as snacks.

To use dried tomatoes, put them in a bowl, pour on boiling water to cover, and let them sit for 10 minutes until soft. Drain, chop as needed, and add to your recipe. You won't need to soak them when making soups and stews, just toss them straight into the pot.

You can also store dried tomatoes in olive oil. It takes them about a week to soften up in the oil, then they will be ready to toss straight into pasta or on a pizza. (If you dip the tomatoes first into a bowl of vinegar, they soften up faster.) Please keep oil-packed tomatoes in the refrigerator, so as not to invite botulism.

ROASTED TOMATO SAUCE

Many of us know the feeling that arrives some time in late August or early September when we realize we may have planted just one or two (or twenty) too many tomato plants which are now dripping with tomatoes. Sliced tomato sandwiches have become passé, gallons of gazpacho have been consumed, every conceivable tomato-related salad has been sampled, and still, they keep ripening! What to do? Roast them!

6 pounds, or so, ripe tomatoes — plum tomatoes are best, but any tomato works

1 large sweet onion, peeled and cut into chunks, or use regular onions, about 1½ cups total

9 to 10 cloves garlic, peeled

1½ cups coarsely chopped carrots (optional)

1½ cups coarsely chopped celery (optional)

¼ to ½ cup olive oil

1 teaspoon salt

1 Tablespoon freshly ground black pepper

½ cup coarsely chopped parsley

½ cup coarsely chopped basil

1½ Tablespoons each: fresh thyme and oregano

6 Tablespoons balsamic vinegar

Core and halve (or quarter if large) the tomatoes. Place in a large roasting pan with the onion chunks, carrots, celery and garlic cloves. They can be crowded a bit, but keep on a single layer. Mix the olive oil, salt, pepper, herbs and vinegar and pour over the vegetables. Roast at 400°F for about 45 minutes, until the tomatoes are a deep golden brown and the other vegetables are soft. Let the vegetables cool, then process briefly in a food processor.

You can purée until smooth for a base for soups and stews or a sauce for pizza, or leave more chunky and mix with pasta. Make sure to use a rubber spatula to scrape all the wonderful bits from the pan. Freeze in 1 or 2 cup portions, or in ice cube trays. (After the sauce is frozen the cubes can be stored in plastic zip-top bags.) Should make about 2 quarts.

Variations: You can include sweet peppers, eggplant or zucchini. Or keep it simple and leave out the herbs, adding them later to suit whatever dish you create mid-winter.

DEBBIE'S ROASTED TOMATO SAUCE

Contributed by Debbie Herbert of Eugene.

4 pounds Roma tomatoes

12+ cloves garlic, lightly smashed

Lots of basil "branches"

Olive oil

Salt and pepper to taste

Oil a large roasting pan or two rimmed cookie sheets. Lay the basil branches and garlic in the pan. Cut the tomatoes in half, cut out the stem core, and gently squeeze out the seeds. Place on top of the basil and garlic, cut side down, packed closely together. Drizzle with olive oil, sprinkle with salt and pepper. Roast at 450°F, until the skins are slightly blackened, about 30 minutes. Pull out the basil. If there is a lot of liquid in the pan, return to the oven for a few minutes, until the juice is reduced. Remove the very charred skins as desired. When cool, chop the tomatoes. Debbie freezes her sauce in 1-quart freezer bags by placing flattened bags of sauce on a pan and freezing them. After they are frozen solid they can be stacked in the freezer.

ROASTED GARLIC PASTE

Beginning in July, garlic is harvested and then cured so that it will store well. We grow a lot of garlic here at Elkdream Farm and it is usually ready to take to market by the end of July. Many types of garlic will store quite happily through the winter, but by spring the bulbs start sending up green sprouts—garlic's way of saying it would really much prefer to be in the ground and growing, thank you very much. You can still eat it, but much of the juice will have dried up and you will need more cloves to get that big flavor hit. Freshly dug garlic, on the other hand, is quite juicy and you don't need much to have it say *Garlic* in whatever you cook.

One way to preserve garlic happily coincides with another way to use it: roasting. Roast a bulb of garlic and it is transformed into a buttery, nutty, mellow version of its former self. (The whole root is called the bulb, or head. When disassembled, the individual pieces are the cloves.) Roasted garlic paste can be spread on crackers, toast, fingers, or whatever. Or it can be mixed into a salad dressing, pasta sauce or pot of soup. Here is how:

Cut garlic bulbs in half horizontally, trying to keep each half intact. Place the halves, cut side down, on a cookie sheet or baking pan that has been well oiled with olive oil. Spread the garlic out so that there is a bit of room around each bulb. Bake at 350°F for 30 to 40 minutes, until the cloves are a rich golden brown on the bottom. Your kitchen will smell heavenly and every person in the house and surrounding environs will appear, asking what is for dinner.

When cool, squeeze the garlic from its wrappers into a small bowl. Add the juices from the pan and mash with a fork. Use immediately or pack the paste into ice cube trays and freeze. Turn the frozen cubes out into a zip-top bag and store in the freezer until called for.

PESTOS AND FROZEN HERBS

There are some herbs that take well to being dried: oregano, sage, thyme and rosemary, for instance. Other soft-leaved herbs lose most of their flavor, or their flavor changes significantly, when dried. Freezing these soft-leaved herbs works very well and makes their bright clean tastes available all year long.

Sprigs of parsley, small bundles of chives, and branches of dill and epazote (a Mexican herb that does miraculous things to a pot of beans) can be frozen whole in little plastic bags. When you need to add them to a recipe, take some out of the bag and chop or crumble them directly into your dish without thawing. It is best not to freeze too much in one bag though, and be sure the herbs are dry before you put them in the freezer, so that you won't have to wrestle with a solid block of herb.

Other tender herbs, such as cilantro and basil, do best when blended with oil to lock in the herbs' essential oils. Chop clean, dry, fresh leaves and tender stems in a food processor with enough vegetable oil or olive oil to visibly coat the chopped herbs (vegetable oil has a more neutral taste, making the cubes amenable to a wider range of recipes). The mixture should be thick and concentrated. Fill ice cube trays with the herb paste and freeze. When frozen, the cubes can be stored in zip-top bags or plastic freezer containers. In most recipes, add the herb cubes toward the end of the cooking time —just as you would fresh herbs—but use about a third as much herb paste as you would fresh herbs (remember it is concentrated). Herb paste is good in soups, stews, salad dressings, basting mixtures and dips.

Some herbs, such as chives, don't need to be put up at all, but will sit happily in a pot on your window sill all winter, ready to be snipped into a winter slaw or sprinkled on a baked potato.

BASIL PESTO

Most of the work in making pesto is in the preparation. It is best if you set aside an entire morning, picking the basil just after the dew has dried (or getting it fresh from the farmers market in the morning) and going immediately into production. I have been known, however, to harvest one day and process the next, and the result is quite satisfactory. Keeping basil in the refrigerator too long is not advisable though, as the leaves begin to turn black and the flavor goes off.

4 cups packed fresh basil leaves

1 cup flat-leaf parsley

1 cup good quality extra virgin olive oil

2 cups freshly grated Parmesan, or half Parmesan and half pecorino Romano

1 cup walnuts

1 teaspoon salt

4 large cloves garlic, peeled

Put the garlic, salt, walnuts and cheese in a food processor and buzz briefly. Add the parsley, basil and oil and process until smooth. Freeze in ¼- to ½-cup containers. Thaw and toss with pasta, or slather on pizza, or add to soup, or spread on crostini, or serve as a dip… the list goes on and on.

CILANTRO PARSLEY PESTO

**2 cups packed cilantro and flat-leaf parsley—
more cilantro or less, according to your preference**

2 cloves garlic

¼ cup olive oil

1 Tablespoon toasted sesame oil

1 Tablespoon lemon juice

Dash tamari sauce

½ teaspoon salt

2 Tablespoons sunflower seeds

½ inch slice of fresh ginger, peeled

Blend in a food processor and use fresh or freeze.
Try with pasta, or as a sauce on steamed vegetables.

DILLY PESTO

2 cups dill fronds

½ cup olive oil

¼ cup walnuts

2 large cloves garlic

¾ cup grated Parmesan or Romano cheese

Process the dill, olive oil, walnuts and garlic in a food processor until well blended. Add the cheese and process for another 10 to 20 seconds, until creamy. Freeze as you would basil pesto. Lovely on fish, tossed with steamed vegetables, or with noodles.

ROASTED PEPPERS FROM STILLPOINT FARM

Lots of red peppers

Olive oil

Preheat the oven to 500°F. Lightly oil a baking sheet. Slice each pepper in half lengthwise and remove the stems, seeds and membranes. Lay the pepper halves cut side down on the baking sheet and brush lightly with olive oil. Roast until the skins darken and blister, about 15 minutes. Remove the peppers from the oven, transfer to a large bowl and cover. The peppers will steam in their own juices. After 10 minutes, slip off the skins. Do not rinse, as the water will dilute the taste. Freeze in freezer bags to use all winter long in lots of yummy recipes, such as combining the peppers with capers, white wine and olive oil for a topping on baked fish.

MORE ABOUT FROZEN ROASTED PEPPERS

Frozen roasted Anaheim peppers are one of the staples that see us through the fall and winter. At the Eugene Saturday Market there is a pepper grower with an ingenious rotating basket suspended over a flame—the aroma of the various peppers roasting on site is quite intoxicating. You can roast your own peppers using the oven-roasting method above, or by placing them on a hot grill until the skins start to blister, turning them until all sides are blackened. Freeze them whole on a cookie sheet, then place in zip-top bags. The skins come off quite easily after a few seconds in the microwave or after defrosting on the counter.

LARS WATSON'S MOTHER'S FAMOUS BREAD AND BUTTER PICKLES

For years, Lars and his wife Lucille had been making these pickles and selling them at auctions at my mother's Unitarian church. One year, my mother bid on and won a pickle-making lesson from them.

4 quarts medium pickling cucumbers, the short warty kind

6 medium onions

2 green sweet bell peppers

1 large head garlic

5 cups granulated sugar

2 teaspoons tumeric

1 Tablespoon celery seed

2 Tablespoons yellow mustard seed

½ cup pickling salt

4 cups organic apple cider vinegar

8 to 10 dill seed heads

Day One: Wash the cucumbers and slice thin. Peel the onions and slice thin. Wash, seed and coarsely chop the peppers. Separate and peel the cloves of garlic. Layer the vegetables in a large non-reactive bowl with salt sprinkled over each layer. Cover with a lot of ice cubes and leave in the refrigerator overnight.

Day Two: Drain, rinse well and drain again. Combine the vinegar, sugar and spices. Bring to a boil in a non-reactive kettle. Make sure the sugar dissolves completely. Add the vegetables and bring to a boil again. Meanwhile, sterilize 8 to 10 pint jars, lids and rims. Distribute the vegetables among the jars and add a dill head to each jar. Add the hot liquid to just within a ½ inch of the top. Release any air bubbles with the blade of a table knife. Wipe the rims clean. Cover and process for 10 minutes in a boiling water bath.

JOANNA'S CARAMEL SPICE PEAR BUTTER

About 15 firm ripe Bartlett pears

2 cups water

6 cups white sugar

1 teaspoon ground cloves

1½ teaspoons ground cinnamon

½ teaspoon ground dry ginger

2 Tablespoons fresh lemon juice

Canola oil

Wash and core, but do not peel, the pears. Slice the pears and put them in a 5-quart pan. Add the water, cover and simmer, until very tender, about 30 minutes.

Let cool slightly. Process in a food processor until finely chopped. Lightly oil the 5-quart pan and return the pears to it.

In a wide heavy frying pan over medium heat, melt 1½ cups of the sugar, stirring often, until it caramelizes to a medium brown syrup. Pour it immediately into the pear pulp. It will sizzle and harden, but will dissolve again as the preserves heat and cook. Stir in the remaining 4½ cups sugar and the spices, blend well.

Bring the mixture to a boil, reduce heat and cook, uncovered, over low heat, until thickened, about 45 minutes. Stir frequently to prevent scorching and sticking. A heat diffuser is very useful. Stir in the lemon juice just before removing from the heat.

Prepare 9 or 10 half-pint jars, rims and caps. Process in a boiling water bath for 10 minutes.

COLD STORAGE

Odd as it may seem, in order to "live", vegetables and fruits continue making energy even after they have been harvested. To do this they continue to break down the carbohydrates, proteins and fats that they created in the garden. Once the carbohydrates, proteins and fats are gone, the vegetable dies and begins the process of decay, at which point you will no longer want to eat it — but your worms will!

This metabolizing process is faster when the air temperature is higher. The goal, then, is to keep your vegetables as cold as possible without injuring them. How cold is that? Veggies generally fall into two camps: those that like it really cold, and those that prefer it just on the cool side. Kale, carrots and beets, for instance, can handle the frigid world of your refrigerator. Tomatoes, eggplants and potatoes, on the other hand, will turn mealy and unappetizing when subjected to refrigeration.

Then there is the humidity factor. Most vegetables prefer that you provide them with some humidity so that they do not shrivel up and wither away. Placing some vegetables in plastic bags or wrapping greens in moist towels will protect them. Onions, garlic and winter squash, however, will rot if you treat them like this; they are much happier when kept in the normal humidity of a closet or cupboard.

Some fruits and vegetables give off a lot of ethylene gas, which causes their neighbors to ripen quickly and can harm celery, cabbage, carrots, potatoes, onions and leafy greens. Take care, then, to loosely close bags of apples in your refrigerator or sequester them in a separate storage location. Traditional wisdom says never store your apples with your potatoes.

Ad hoc root cellars can be created in outside storage sheds or garages. *Root Cellaring* by Mike and Nancy Bubel is full of ideas on how to create these storage spaces that were once commonplace.

Most refrigerators hover around 35–40°F, and unheated basements, if you are lucky enough to have one, average around 60°F. Here is a quick list of who likes it cold and humid, and who likes it cool and dry.

Apples: Store apples in a box or bin in a cool dark location — ideally at 34°F with 90% humidity. They store best when separated a bit — many people wrap them individually in a sheet of newsprint. Make sure you don't put any bruised apples in with the keepers (not for nothing do they say one bad apple will spoil the whole bunch!). Some apples will keep 3 to 5 months in optimal conditions.

Cabbage and Brussels Sprouts: Keep them cold and humid, like roots. You can store cabbage on a shelf in the root cellar or piled in a cold corner of a porch or detached garage, covered with straw or leaves. For Brussels sprouts, remove the leaves and store the stalks like cabbage — they'll keep a month or so.

Leeks: I keep my leeks in the garden all winter, but you can also trim their leaves and pack them upright in a plastic pail with a few inches of soil at the bottom. Add water to keep the soil moist. They like it cold and humid.

Onions, Shallots and Garlic: Keep these cold, like roots, but not as humid. Use boxes with some ventilation or onion bags.

Potatoes: Keep in a dark cold (no lower than 45°F) humid location.

Root Vegetables and Tubers: Carrots, parsnips and other root vegetables can be stored in plastic bags in your refrigerator or in plastic pails in a root cellar or cold location — best at 31–33°F with high humidity. You don't want them to dry out, but you also don't want them to have visible water droplets, lest they rot. If you put them in a plastic pail, monitor the moisture weekly, regulating it with the lid position more or less ajar. Give the roots a bit of space, rather than packing them tightly. For instance, lay out a loose layer of parallel carrots with the next layer placed in a perpendicular direction.

Squash and Pumpkins: Keep them cool (50–60°F) and rather dry. They don't mind sitting on the floor in an unused closet or room.

Tomatoes: Keep them cool (45–65°F) and humid (80%+).

GOING MORE LOCAL

So you have committed to giving up peaches in February. You are buying locally grown lettuce, you are growing your own tomatoes and freezing berries by the bucketful. What's next?

Well... wheat. Or grains in general. Wheat, corn and oats are such staples in our diets. But many fields that once provided the Pacific Northwest with grain are now planted with grass seed, and the local mills that once ground the grain have been torn down or converted to other uses, making it more challenging to relocalize this part of our diet.

According to David Stelzer of Azure Standard, rye, spelt, triticale, soft white wheat and teff are already being grown in the Oregon-Washington area. There are other grains, like barley and oats, that are also grown locally, but during the hulling process they are mixed with product that comes from outside the region. Stalford Farms in Tangent, Oregon, however, has just started harvesting a hard red wheat that can be used in making bread. This is the beginning of an exciting joint effort, with Ten Rivers Food Web, to relocalize the food system.

Even if you can't find grains that have been grown in your watershed, try purchasing bulk grain and making your own granola, or cooking up a pot of hot cereal in the morning, instead of buying boxed cereal. Although the grains may not have been grown locally, you will be eating a bowl of cereal that has undergone less processing, and has less packaging, than a box of commercial cereal.

OUR FAVORITE GRANOLA

1½ pounds regular rolled oats

½ pound quick oats

½ cup wheat germ

½ cup sunflower seeds

½ cup chopped almonds

¾ cup honey

¾ cup canola oil

1 teaspoon vanilla (optional)

In a large bowl, toss together the dry ingredients. Combine the oil and honey in a glass measuring cup or bowl and heat briefly in a saucepan (or microwave), so that they mix more easily. Add the vanilla (if using). Toss with the oat mixture—I usually end up working it with my hands—making sure the dry ingredients are well coated. Spread on a large rimmed cookie sheet (or divide between two sheets) and cook in a 300°F oven. Stir every 5 or 10 minutes. Bake a total of 20 to 30 minutes, until the granola is golden, but not too brown. Cool and store in a glass or plastic container.

Variations: Try mixing a teaspoon of ground cardamom with the oats. Or sprinkle in some ground ginger and cinnamon or nutmeg.

WHOLE GRAIN SALADS

Wheat berries make a wonderful salad. Rye berries can be substituted for wheat berries, as can triticale berries.

2 cups wheat, rye or triticale berries

6 cups water

Dressing

Chopped Nuts (walnuts, hazelnuts, almonds, pine nuts)

Cheese (feta cheese, goat cheese, coarsely grated Parmesan)

Dried fruit (raisins, currants, dried cranberries)

Greens or steamed vegetables (fresh spinach, lightly steamed kale or chard, blanched broccoli, fresh or frozen peas)

Combine the berries and water in a large saucepan and bring to a boil. Lower the heat to a simmer and cook for an hour or so, until the berries are plump and chewy. You may need to add more water. The only way to check for doneness is to taste a few berries.

Toss the hot berries with your dressing of choice and add the chopped nuts, cheese and greens. For instance, try dried cranberries plus toasted walnuts plus torn spinach leaves (the hot berries will wilt the spinach) in the fall. Or combine steamed pieces of asparagus, slivered almonds and goat cheese in the spring. Pine nuts, feta and steamed green beans would be tasty in the summer. Experiment!

BEANS, GREENS & GRAINS

Canned beans in the pantry make it easy to throw together a batch of Beans, Greens & Grains, but if you have time, try cooking up some locally grown dried beans. Fresh dried beans, (i.e., beans that have not been sitting in the store for many months) cook very fast and have more flavor than canned beans.

1½ cups dried beans, cooked, or 1 can beans (kidney, cannellini, black, adzuki, etc.)

1 to 2 cups cooked whole grain, such as kasha (toasted buckwheat), quinoa, barley or wild rice

1 small onion, chopped

1 to 2 cloves garlic, minced

½ pound greens, such as cabbage, kale, chard, mustard greens, spinach or a combination, tough stems removed and leaves roughly chopped

½ cup parsley

1 cup vegetable stock

3 to 4 ounces crumbled feta cheese or grated Parmesan cheese

Sauté the onion and garlic in a large frying pan until soft. Add the greens and cook until just tender. Add the beans, parsley, salt and pepper, and stock. Simmer until the greens are completely tender. Fold in the cooked grains. Garnish with the feta or Parmesan.

Additional twists: Add sautéed mushrooms, canned or dried tomatoes, or toasted nuts. Other fresh herbs might include cilantro, basil, oregano or thyme.

HERBAL TEAS

There is a dizzying array of boxed herbal teas to be found in any grocery store. But many herbs are grown locally—perhaps as close by as your own garden—and very easy to dry. If you have a patch of mint growing, cut a bunch of branches, bundle them with a rubber band, and hang them upside down to dry. When they are brittle, strip the leaves off the stems and store in a glass jar. Try different combinations of mints. Chamomile is also easy to grow. Sage is lovely when made into tea. Lemon thyme is good in tea too. You don't need to dry herbs before you make tea with them. A tisane, or fresh herb tea, can be made by placing a good handful of fresh herbs in a teapot and covering them with boiling water. Let it steep 5 to 10 minutes, then strain into mugs. Or chill and drink the tea on ice.

LOCALLY RAISED MEATS AND SUSTAINABLY HARVESTED SEAFOOD

At this time, locally grown meats are more expensive than the prepackaged industrially raised meats sold in the grocery store. If you are only looking at the price at the cash register, that is. The long-term costs to the environment, and to your health, significantly raise the price of a pack of chicken thighs or baby back ribs. According to a recent report by the United Nations, livestock production is responsible for 18% of the world's human-caused greenhouse gas emissions. The carbon dioxide portion of these emissions comes from deforestation and other degradations to the land in the pursuit of ever more grazing and feed production acreage, as well as from the fossil fuels used to refrigerate, transport and fertilize crops for animal fodder. Raising livestock solely in the pasture, however, produces far less greenhouse gas emissions, and happily, the animals digest their food better, resulting in less methane gas emissions (which is to say, when not raised on the pasture land they are biologically predisposed to subsist on, cows and other four-legged beasts tend to become flatulent, resulting in, simply put, an excess of burping and farting). Try to eat meat less often, and eat less of it when you do serve it. Simply cutting the amount of meat in your diet from 35% to 20% of your caloric intake can have the same impact on global warming as switching from driving a Toyota Camry to a Prius! If you choose local pasture-fed meat, the impact on our planet will be all the less. Meat can be used as a flavoring, or as a side dish, with vegetables and whole grains taking a starring role in your meal plan. It's better for you, and better for your world!

Industrially-farmed seafood can also be hazardous to the environment, and not much better for your health. Consider the following facts:

- Farmed fish are given more antibiotics per pound than any other type of livestock.

- Pink dye is added to the fish pellets fed to farmed salmon; otherwise, their flesh would be grey.

- Industrial fish farms can be viewed as the equivalent of floating hog or poultry farms. Some farms dump into the sea, every day, an amount of sewage that is equal to that generated by a city of a million people.

- Farm-raised salmon is 50% higher in unhealthy fats and lower in Omega 3 fatty acids than wild salmon.

- Farmed salmon eat pellets made from mackerel, sardines and other small fish. It takes nearly 2½ pounds of small fish to raise one pound of farmed fish.

What to do? Simply switching to wild-caught fish is not enough, given that today's fleets of industrial trawlers (massive vessels that scrape up huge swaths of the ocean floor) and long-liners (boats that drag hooked lines that can measure up to several miles in length) have fished out at least 90% of the world's large ocean fish (tuna, marlin, swordfish, shark, cod, halibut, skates and flounder). Instead, seek out fish that have been caught in nearby coastal waters by fishermen who use hand lines or other sustainable fishing methods. Research which fish stocks are in danger of being fished out. Download the handy wallet-sized information card from Monterey Bay Aquarium's Seafood Watch at **http://www.montereybayaquarium.org/cr/cr_seafoodwatch/download.asp**. Ask your grocer to carry and identify sustainably harvested seafood. Ask your favorite chef to do the same.

SWEETENERS

Seek out local honey producers. You'll be amazed at how different honeys can taste, depending on which local flowers the bees have been sipping from. And contrary to what we have been led to believe, the syrup you pour over your weekend pancakes or waffles does not have to always be maple. There are many scrumptious fruit syrups made locally from the wonderful berries that grow in our region. You can find them at many stores and farmers markets, or you can harvest your own blackberries and make your own syrup!

DAIRY PRODUCTS AND EGGS

Artisan cheeses are extremely popular at the moment, and there has been a wonderful increase in the number of people making cheeses from locally raised goats and cows. Look for locally crafted cheeses in farmers markets and specialty grocery stores. You might also find milk from nearby dairies.

Locally raised eggs can be purchased as well, sometimes in surprising locations—like your neighborhood feed or hardware store. Or build a small coop and get yourself a few laying hens!

REFERENCES

Following are some of the many books I have been inspired by, both in terms of the importance of eating local foods, and the many ways to cook them. I must confess to being a notorious hoarder of recipes. For years I have been scribbling ideas for ingredients and cooking techniques out of countless magazines and newspapers. I therefore would like to credit the many other cooks out there whose recipes have been a wellspring of inspiration. May all of us who dance gleefully around the kitchen waving our wooden spoons in the air when a recipe turns out well continue to trade new ideas for feeding family and friends.

Abelman, Michael. *Fields of Plenty*. San Francisco: Chronicle Books, 2005.

Berry, Wendell. *What Are People For?* New York: North Point Press, 1990.

Burros, Marian. "Food-Borne Illness from Produce on the Rise" *New York Times* (23 November 2003).

Coleman, Eliot. *The New Organic Grower's Four-Season Harvest*. Vermont: Chelsea Green Publishing Company, 1992.

Cool, Jesse Ziff. *Your Organic Kitchen: The Essential Guide to Selecting and Cooking Organic Foods*. Pennsylvania: Rodale Press, 2000.

Della Croce, Julia. *The Classic Italian Cookbook*. New York: DK Publishing, Inc., 1996.

Goodall, Jane, Gary McAvoy, and Gail Hudson. *Harvest for Hope: A Guide to Mindful Eating*. New York: Warner Books, 2005.

Greene, Janet, Ruth Hertzberg and Beatrice Vaughan. *Putting Food By*. Vermont: Stephen Greene Press, 1973.

Gussow, Joan Dye. "Dietary Guidelines for Sustainability" *Journal of Nutrition Education*, Volume 18, Number 1, 1986.

Gussow, Joan Dye. *This Organic Life: Confessions of a Suburban Homesteader.* White River Junction, Vermont: Chelsea Green, 2002.

Halweil, Brian. *Eat Here: Homegrown Pleasures in a Global Supermarket.* New York: W.W. Norton & Company, 2004.

Hibler, Janie. *Dungeness Crabs and Blackberry Cobblers: The Northwest Heritage Cookbook.* New York: Alfred A. Knopf, Inc., 1991.

Hirsch, David. *The Moosewood Restaurant Kitchen Garden: Creative Gardening for the Adventurous Cook.* New York: Fireside, 1992.

Katzen, Mollie. *The Moosewood Cookbook: Recipes from Moosewood Restaurant.* Berkeley, California: Ten Speed Press, 1977.

Katzen, Mollie. *Still Life with Menu Cookbook.* Berkeley, CA: Ten Speed Press, 1988.

Kingsolver, Barbara, Steven L. Hopp and Camille Kingsolver. *Animal, Vegetable, Miracle: A Year of Food Life.* New York: HarperCollins Books, 2007.

Lappe, Frances Moore, and Anna Lappe. *Hope's Edge: The Next Diet for a Small Planet.* New York: Jeremy P. Tarcher, 2003.

Long, Cheryl. "More Evidence that Food Nutrient Quality is Declining," *Mother Earth News Almanac* (April/May 2005).

Madison, Deborah. *Greens: Extraordinary Vegetarian Cuisine from the Celebrated Restaurant.* New York: Bantam Books, 1987.

Madison, Deborah. *Local Flavors.* New York: Broadway Books, 2002.

McKibben, Bill. "The Cuba Diet" *Harpers Magazine* (April 2005).

Murray, Sarah. "The Deep Fried Truth" *New York Times* (14 December 2007).

Nabhan, Gary Paul. *Coming Home to Eat: The Pleasures and Politics of Local Foods*. New York: W.W. Norton & Company, 2002.

Ogden, Shepherd and Ellen. *The Cooks Garden*. Pennsylvania: Rodale Press, 1989.

Pierce, Neal. "Time to Become a Locavore" *Seattle Times* (9 October 2006).

Pollan, Michael. "Mass Natural" *New York Times* (4 June 2006).

Pollan, Michael. "Our Decrepit Food Factories" *New York Times* (16 December 2007).

Pollan, Michael. "Unhappy Meals" *New York Times* (28 January 2007).

Pollan, Michael. *The Omnivore's Dilemma: A Natural History of Four Meals*. New York: Penguin, 2006.

Reinhart, Br. Peter. *Sacramental Magic in a Small-Town Café: Recipes and Stories from Brother Juniper's Café*. New York: Addison-Wesley Publishing Company, 1994.

Smith, Alisa and J.B. MacKinnon. *Plenty: One Man, One Woman and a Raucous Year of Eating Locally*. New York: Harmony Books 2007.

Starke, Linda, et al. *State of the World 2004*. New York-London: W.W. Norton & Company, 2004.

Traunfeld, Jerry. *The Herbfarm Cookbook*. New York: Scribner, 2000.

Viestad, Andreas. *Kitchen of Light*. New York: Workman Publishing, 2003.

CONTRIBUTORS

The following restaurants, farms and individuals have contributed recipes to this book:

Groundwork Organics Farm is a seventy-five acre farm north of Eugene, along the Willamette River in Junction City. They grow a wide variety of fruits and vegetables for sale at farmers markets and for their Community Supported Agriculture program. In addition they offer wholesale delivery to Eugene and Portland twice weekly, supplying many of the area's best restaurants and markets. All acreage is Oregon Tilth certified organic.

Hey Bayles! Farm is a family-run certified-organic farm growing a wide range of fruits and vegetables and specializing in leafy greens. They currently work 12 acres in the Oregon Coast Range and distribute high quality produce through their Community Supported Agriculture program, at the Lane County Farmers Market, Eugene's best natural food stores, and in many outstanding restaurants.

Marché Restaurant's focus is on celebrating life and the bountiful Pacific Northwest with locally grown and gathered food, prepared with care, and served in a lively and elegant atmosphere. The menu is based on the foods you would find at a farmers market — fresh seasonal and regional. They are committed to using only those ingredients that are at their best, so the menu evolves throughout the seasons.

River Bend Farm and Pleasant Hill Orchard is a 25-plus acre, family-owned and operated farm located on the Coast Fork of the Willamette River. They specialize in orchard fruits, strawberries, hazelnuts, cane berries and vegetables. They also sell an array of baked goods.

Stillpoint Farm specializes in berries from May through November, offered either u-pick or freshly picked. They also offer a wide variety of traditional and unusual produce, like okra, which they grow in a greenhouse, as it is not otherwise inclined to thrive in the Pacific Northwest.

Sweetwater Farm and Nursery, located 7 miles west of Creswell, has been growing organic produce for 28 years. Their farmers grow vegetables, raspberries, mushrooms, free-range eggs and grass-fed beef. 150 families receive weekly food shares through their Community Supported Agriculture program. They are concerned with the re-mineralization of the soil, which affects the nutritional density of the produce. They truly believe "Health comes from the farm, not the pharmacy."

Wintergreen Farm is a two-family farm in the foothills of the Coast Range, 20 miles west of Eugene. Their crops have been Oregon Tilth certified organic since 1984. They produce a wide diversity of vegetables, herbs and small fruits, as well as raising horses and beef cattle.

The following individuals have generously contributed their recipes and inspiration:

Paula Chambers	**Bill Mumbach**
Joanna England	**Barb Shaw**
Lynne Fessenden	**Marijo Taylor**
Debbie Herbert	**Jake Walsh**
Jude Hobbs	

LOCAL RESOURCES

Who can you call for more information? Below is a list of some of the community resources that I have utilized. There are many others—this is by no means an exhaustive listing!

Willamette Farm & Food Coalition publishes a wonderful yearly directory of farms, wineries and restaurants providing locally grown food to the Willamette Valley. In addition, it has charts of when produce is available, lists of resources, a calendar of events, and numerous other great tidbits of information.

Willamette Farm & Food Coalition
1192 Lawrence Street, Eugene OR 97401
541-341-1216
info@lanefood.org
www.lanefood.org

Eugene Permaculture Guild sponsors a number of events throughout the year that are helpful to those of us interested in learning more about how to feed ourselves.

Eugene Permaculture Guild
Jan Spencer
541-686-6761
www.eugenepermacultureguild.org

Lane County Extension Service. If you have a question about canning, can't figure out what is eating your bean leaves, or are interested in learning how to become a master gardener, call these wonderfully helpful people!

Lane County Extension Service
950 W 13th Avenue, Eugene OR 97402
541-682-4246
http://extension.oregonstate.edu/land

Oregon Tilth publishes a monthly newsletter full of great information on sustainable farming and gardening, and connected tilth organizations. They sponsor regular events and meetings throughout the Willamette Valley.

Oregon Tilth
470 Lancaster Drive NE, Salem OR 97301
503-378-0690
www.tilth.org

Slow Food Eugene. Get involved with people who love to spend time cooking and eating the old-fashioned way: slowly and with great pleasure.

Slow Food Eugene
Tom Barkin
541-343-2619
Eugene@slowfoodusa.org
www.slowfoodeugene.org

Ten Rivers Food Web was formed by folks in Benton, Linn and Lincoln counties who wanted to strengthen local food security and make locally raised foods more available.

Ten Rivers Food Web
www.tenriversfoodweb.org

HELPFUL WEBSITES

Here are a few websites that I have explored and found to be helpful. New sites pop up almost daily, but these sites were still active as of October 2008.

The 100 Mile Diet. **www.100milediet.org** A website started by Alisa Smith and J.B. MacKinnon, authors of *Plenty*, the book detailing their year of eating only what food could be obtained within a hundred mile radius of their home in Vancouver, B.C. The website has stories from people all over the world interested in eating locally, lots of suggestions for how to make your diet more sustainable, and a mapping tool to help you figure out the parameters of your local foodshed.

Chef's Collaborative. **www.chefscollaborative.org** A national network of chefs, food producers, educators and food lovers who come together to celebrate local foods and foster a more sustainable food supply. On their site you can find restaurants all over the country that serve locally grown foods.

Cook Here and Now. **www.cookhereandnow.com** The blog of an Italian cook hailing originally from Rome. He posts regular installments of recipes, tips and anecdotes on cooking and eating locally. He is based in the San Francisco Bay Area, but a lot of the information can be applied to the Pacific Northwest.

Eat Local. **www.EatLocal.net** An extremely informative, easy-to-use website with links to many great resources across the U.S. It also has lots of great recipes, inspiring articles and lots of support for those who want to make their diet more sustainable.

Eat Well Guide. **www.eatwellguide.org** A guide for finding fresh, wholesome, sustainable food in the U.S. and Canada. The site lists farms, stores, restaurants and outlets.

Edible Communities. **www.ediblecommunities.com** Their mission is to transform the way communities shop for, cook, eat, and relate to the food that is grown and produced. Through printed publications, websites, and events, they connect consumers, from a variety of regions across the country, with local growers, retailers, chefs, and food artisans, enabling those relationships to grow and thrive in a mutually beneficial, healthful, and economically viable way.

Edible Portland. **www.edibleportland.com** A magazine and website serving Portland and the Willamette Valley. They publish seasonal recipes, lists of events, and a listing of businesses that feature local seasonal products and services in the Portland area.

Seasonal Cornucopia. **www.seasonalcornucopia.com** This amazing website makes it possible to search for available foods in each season. It is based in the Puget Sound region of Washington.

Sustainable Table. **www.sustainabletable.org** Another site with a plethora of tasty sounding recipes. Would that I had time to cook them all!

Urban Edibles. **http://.urbanedibles.org** An intriguing site created by a cooperative network of wild food foragers. Based in Portland, their ideas could well be expanded to include other areas. The site includes a map of where in Portland one can find various wild edibles, plus information on identifying and harvesting edible and medicinal plants, preservation techniques, and other useful tidbits.

INDEX

APPLES
Apple Pie with Sage, 180
Baked Apples with Lingonberries, 81
Cabbage and Apple Salad, 48
Fresh Pear/Apple Crumble Pie, 178
Ginger Baked Apples, 177
Storage, 204
Winter Salads, 46

ASPARAGUS
Asparagus with Mushrooms and Rice, 98
Cream of Asparagus Soup, 95
Ginger-Marinated Asparagus, 106
Spring Season Features, 85

ARTICHOKES
Spring Season Features, 85

ARUGULA
Beet and Arugula Salad with Fresh Chèvre, 91
Spring Frittata, 100

BARLEY
Barley and Lentil Soup with Swiss Chard, 151
Beans, Greens & Grains, 208

BEANS, DRIED
Beans, Greens & Grains, 208
Bean Soup Mix, 50
Fall Stew, 165
Mexican Veggie Pot Pie, 132
Mighty Fine Bean Soup, 51
Minestrone, 152
White Bean Dip, 43
White Bean, Squash, Kale and Olive Stew, 158

BEANS, FAVA
Fava Bean Crostini, 88
Fava Bean Salad, 92

BEANS, GREEN
Dilly Beans, 199
Green Bean Tomato Curry, 136
Groundwork Organic's Favorite Veggie Melt, 131
Minestrone, 152
Oil-Roasted Green Beans, Potatoes and Fennel, 137
Summer Season Features, 115

BEEF
Joanna's Beef Stew, 58
Stifado, 60

BEETS
Beet and Arugula Salad with Fresh Chèvre, 91
Baby Beet Salad, 93
Mid-Winter Vegetable Cure, 66
Raw Beet Salad, 148
Roast Beets with Thyme and Garlic, 108
Spring Season Features, 85

BERRIES
Berry Good Sauce, 138
Blackberry Butter, 177
Blackberry Cobbler, 139
Blackberry Sauce for Salmon, 164
Dried Strawberries, 190
Frozen, 190
Frozen Berry Crisp, 79
Mixed Fruit Compote, 80

BOK CHOI
Pad Thai, 129
Sesame Braised Bok Choi, 169

BURDOCK
Fall Season Features, 144
Kinpira, 145

BROCCOLI
Groundwork Organic's Favorite
　Veggie Melt, 131
Lemon-Garlic Broccoli, 175
Spring Season Features, 86

BRUSSELS SPROUTS
Curried Tofu and Vegetables, 56
Fall Season Features, 143
Storage, 204

BULGAR WHEAT
Bulgar and Winter Vegetables, 59
Tabbouli, 125

CABBAGE
Aunt Stel's Piccalilli, 200
Cabbage and Apple Salad, 48
Coleslaw with Ginger-Mustard
　Dressing, 149
Curried Tofu and Vegetables, 56
Fall Season Features, 144
Minestrone, 152
Spicy Red Cabbage, 75
Sri Lankan Cabbage, 73
Storage, 204
Unbelievably Good Coleslaw, 47
Wintergreen Farm Cabbage Slaw, 49
Winter Salads, 46

CARROTS
Carrot and Turnip Pancakes, 72
Carrot Ginger Soup, 55
Carrots with Ginger and
　Cardamom, 71
Coleslaw with Ginger-Mustard
　Dressing, 149
Curried Winter Vegetable Soup, 52
Kinpira, 145
Kohlrabi and Carrot Salad, 150
Mashed Rutabaga, 67
Mid-Winter Vegetable Cure, 66
Potarrots, 67
Risotto with Onions, Carrots
　and Fennel, 135
Roast Roots, 172

Storage, 204
Winter Season Features, 39
Wintergreen Farm Cabbage Slaw, 49
Unbelievably Good Coleslaw, 47

CAULIFLOWER
Cauliflower with Cumin and
　Cheese, 68
Curried Tofu and Vegetables, 56
Winter Season Features, 39

CELERIAC
Bulgar and Winter Vegetables, 59
Celeriac and Potato Purée, 74
Winter Season Features, 39

CELERY
Aunt Stel's Piccalilli, 200

CELERY ROOT, see Celeriac

CHICKEN
Chicken Pot Pie, 62
English Shepherd's Pie, 64

COLLARDS
Dave's Savory Collard Greens, 69
Winter Season Features, 39

223

CORN
Frozen, 190
Good Corn Bread, 133
Hominy, in Fall Stew, 165
Mexican Corn, 134
Polenta, 167
Salmon and Corn Chowder, 54
Summer Season Features, 115

CRANBERRIES
Cranberry Sauce for Grilled or
   Poached Salmon, 163
Sunday Morning Muffins, 77

CUCUMBERS
Gazpacho, 126
Lars Watson's Mother's Famous Bread
   and Butter Pickles, 201
Summer Season Features, 115
Tabbouli, 125

CROSTINI AND BRUSCHETTA
Claudia's Mushroom Crostini, 45
Claudia's Summer Crostini, 118
Eggplant Bruschetta, 119
Fava Bean Crostini, 88

EDAMAME
Summer Season Features, 116

EGGS
Spring Frittata, 100

EGGPLANT
Eggplant Bruschetta, 119
Ratatouille with Polenta, 166
Stillpoint Farm's Grilled or
   Broiled Japanese Eggplant, 134
Summer Season Features, 116

FENNEL, BULBING
Fall Season Features, 144
Mid-Winter Vegetable Cure, 66
Oil-Roasted Green Beans, Potatoes
   and Fennel, 137
Risotto with Onions, Carrots and
   Fennel, 135
Roast Roots, 172
Winter Vegetable Gratin, 61

FETA CHEESE
Pasta Salad with Tomato and
   Feta Cheese, 122

FISH, SALMON
Blackberry Sauce for Salmon, 164
Cranberry Sauce for Grilled or
   Poached Salmon, 163
Mom's Favorite Salmon Chowder, 53
Northwest Noodles, 102
Peder's Favorite Salmon Marinade, 164
Salmon and Corn Chowder, 54

FISH, TUNA
Pasta with Kale Rabe and Tuna, 103

FRUIT, DRIED
Baked Breakfast Pudding, 78
Mixed Fruit Compote, 80
Sunday Morning Muffins, 77

FRUIT, FROZEN
Frozen Berry Crisp, 79
Mixed Fruit Compote, 80

GARLIC
Green, in Spring Season Features, 86
Roast Beets with Thyme and
   Garlic, 108
Roasted Garlic Paste, frozen, 194
Storage, 204
Whistles, in Spring Season
   Features, 86

GOAT CHEESE
Eggplant Bruschetta, 119
Potato and Chard Bake, 157
Spring Frittata, 100

GREENS, WINTER
Beans, Greens & Grains, 208
Bulgar and Winter Vegetables, 59
Calzone, 156
Pasta with Sausages and Greens, 65
Pizza with Greens, 187
Polenta with Greens, 168
Tempato Patties, 162
Winter Season Features, 41

GREENS, WILD SPRING
Spring Season Features, 87

HAZELNUTS
Bartlett Pear Salad with Rogue
  Creamery Blue Cheese, 147
Hazelnut Blackberry Pancakes, 176
Northwest Noodles, 102

HERBS, see also Pesto
Frozen, 195
Tea, 209

JERUSALEM ARTICHOKES
Winter Season Features, 40

KALE
Farm Style Braised Kale, 70
Kale Salad, 46
Pasta with Kale Rabe and Tuna, 103
Polenta with Greens, 168
Winter Season Features, 39

KASHA
Beans, Greens & Grains, 208

KOHLRABI
Kohlrabi and Carrot Salad, 150
Kohlrabi and Sungold Tomato
  Salad, 148
Kohlrabi Fritters with Fresh
  Herbs, 107
Mid-Winter Vegetable Cure, 66
White Bean, Squash, Kale and
  Olive Stew, 158
Winter Season Features, 40
Winter Salads, 46

LEEKS
Fall Season Features, 144
Potato Leek Soup, 96
Storage, 204

LENTILS
Barley and Lentil Soup with
  Swiss Chard, 151
Lentils with Butter and Parsley, 101

LINGONBERRIES
Baked Apples with Lingonberries, 81

MUFFINS
Sunday Morning Muffins, 77

MUSHROOMS
Asparagus with Mushrooms and
  Rice, 98
Claudia's Mushroom Crostini, 45
Fall Season Features, 144
Polenta with Greens, 168

OATS
Baked Breakfast Pudding, 78
Frozen Berry Crisp, 79
Our Favorite Granola, 206
Pear Crisp, 179
Rhubarb Crisp, 109

ONIONS
Aunt Stel's Piccalilli, 200
Bill Mumbach's Fresh Sweet Onion
  Rings with Basil, 120
Lars Watson's Mother's Famous
  Bread and Butter Pickles, 201
Risotto with Onions, Carrots
  and Fennel, 135
Storage, 204

PARSLEY
Parsley Sauce, 66

PARSNIPS
Bulgar and Winter Vegetables, 59
Curried Winter Vegetable Soup, 52
Roasted Parsnips, 70
Roast Roots, 172
Storage, 204
Winter Season Features, 40

PASTA AND NOODLES
Baked Tomato Spaghetti, 127
Northwest Noodles, 102
Pad Thai, 129
Pasta Salad with Tomato and
  Feta Cheese, 122
Pasta with Kale Rabe and Tuna, 103

Pasta with Sausages and Greens, 65
Swiss Chard with Currants
    and Walnuts, 155

PEARS
Bartlett Pear Salad with Rogue
    Creamery Blue Cheese, 147
Fresh Pear/Apple Crumble Pie, 178
Joanna's Caramel Spice Pear Butter, 202
Pear Crisp, 179

PEAS
Spring Season Features, 86
Wheat Berry Salad with Fresh
    Peas, 94

PEPPERS
Aunt Stel's Piccalilli, 200
Frozen Roasted Peppers, 198
Gazpacho, 126
Lars Watson's Mother's Famous
    Bread and Butter Pickles, 201
Mexican Veggie Pot Pie, 132
Ratatouille with Polenta, 166
Red Devil Squash Creole, 128
Roasted Peppers from Stillpoint
    Farm, 198
Sally's Favorite Sausage and
    Peppers, 159
White Bean, Squash, Kale and
    Olive Stew, 158

PESTO
Basil Pesto, 196
Cilantro Pesto, 197
Dilly Pesto, 197
Dried Tomato Pesto, 146
Pesto and Fresh Tomato Pizza, 186
Pesto Log, 44
Pesto Pizza, 185

PIES
Apple Pie with Sage, 180
Chicken Pot Pie, 62
English Shepherd's Pie, 64
Jake's Tofu-Turkey Pie, 104
Mexican Veggie Pot Pie, 132

PIZZAS AND CALZONES
Calzone, 156
The Kids Favorite Pizza, 185
Pizza Crust, 184
Pesto and Fresh Tomato Pizza, 186
Pesto Pizza, 185
Pizza with Greens, 187
Zucchini and Basil Pizza, 186

PORK
Asian-Style Honey Glazed
    Ribs, 130

POTATOES
Carrot and Turnip Pancakes, 72
Celeriac and Potato Purée, 74
Chard and Potato Enchiladas, 160
Curried Winter Vegetable Soup, 52
English Shepherd's Pie, 64
Fall Stew, 165
Farmor's Potato Salad, 123
Groundwork Organic's Favorite
    Veggie Melt, 131
Mashed Rutabaga, 67
Oil-Roasted Green Beans,
    Potatoes and Fennel, 137
Potarrots, 67
Potato and Chard Bake, 157
Potato Leek Soup, 96
Roast Roots, 172
Storage, 204
Tempato Patties, 162
Winter Vegetable Gratin, 61

POTATOES, SWEET
Winter Vegetable Gratin, 61

QUINOA
Beans, Greens & Grains, 208
in Tabbouli, 125

RADISHES
Spring Season Features, 86

ROOT VEGETABLES, see also Beets; Burdock; Carrots; Celeriac; Kohlrabi; Parsnips; Potatoes; Potatoes, Sweet; Rutabaga; Turnips
Bulgar and Winter Vegetables, 59
Roast Roots, 172
Storage, 204

RHUBARB
Marijo's Rhubarb Cake, 111
Rhubarb Crisp, 109
Rhubarb Sauce, 110

RICE
Asparagus with Mushrooms and Rice, 98
Beans, Greens & Grains, 208
Green Rice, 97
Risotto with Onions, Carrots and Fennel, 135
Stuffed Squash, 174

RUTABAGA
Mashed Rutabaga, 67
Winter Season Features, 41
Winter Vegetable Gratin, 61

SAGE
Winter Squash with Cider Glaze and Sage Butter, 76

SALADS AND SLAWS
Baby Beet Salad, 93
Bartlett Pear Salad with Rogue Creamery Blue Cheese, 147
Beet and Arugula Salad with Fresh Chèvre, 91
Cabbage and Apple Salad, 48
Coleslaw with Ginger-Mustard Dressing, 149
Farmor's Potato Salad, 123
Fava Bean Salad, 92
Kale Salad, 46
Kohlrabi and Carrot Salad, 150
Kohlrabi and Sungold Tomato Salad, 148
Natasha's Venezuelan Boyfriend's Aunt's Green Salad, 124
Pasta Salad with Tomato and Feta Cheese, 122
Raw Beet Salad, 148
Tabbouli, 125
Tomatoes Lutèce, 121
Ultimate Tossed Green Salad, 90
Unbelievably Good Coleslaw, 47
Wheat Berry Salad with Fresh Peas, 94
Whole Grain Salads, 207
Wintergreen Farm Cabbage Slaw, 49
Winter Salads, 46

SAUSAGE
Pasta with Sausages and Greens, 65
Sally's Favorite Sausage and Peppers, 159

SOUPS
Barley and Lentil Soup with Swiss Chard, 151
Carrot Ginger Soup, 55
Cream of Asparagus Soup, 95
Curried Winter Vegetable Soup, 52
Gazpacho, 126
Mighty Fine Bean Soup, 51
Minestrone, 152
Mom's Favorite Salmon Chowder, 53
Potato Leek Soup, 96
Real Deal Cream of Tomato Soup, 154
Salmon and Corn Chowder, 54
Winter Soups, 50

SPINACH
Bulgar and Winter Vegetables, 59
Green Rice, 97
Spinach with Sesame Dressing (Horenso no Goma-Ae), 105

SQUASH, SUMMER
Groundwork Organic's Favorite Veggie Melt, 131
Mexican Veggie Pot Pie, 132
Ratatouille with Polenta, 166
Red Devil Squash Creole, 128
Sage-Roasted Summer Squash, 137
Summer Season Features, 116

SQUASH, WINTER
Curried Tofu and Vegetables, 56
Fall Stew, 165
Stuffed Squash, 174
Squash Pancakes, 170
Squished Squash, 173
Storage, 204
White Bean, Squash, Kale and
   Olive Stew, 158
Winter Season Features, 41
Winter Squash with Cider Glaze
   and Sage Butter, 76
Winter Vegetable Gratin, 61

STEWS
Fall Stew, 165
Joanna's Beef Stew, 58
Ratatouille with Polenta, 166
Stifado, 60
White Bean, Squash, Kale and
   Olive Stew, 158

SWISS CHARD
Barley and Lentil Soup with
   Swiss Chard, 151
Chard and Potato Enchiladas, 160
Polenta with Greens, 168
Potato and Chard Bake, 157
Swiss Chard with Currants and
   Walnuts, 155

TEMPEH
Tempato Patties, 162

TOFU
Curried Tofu and Vegetables, 56
Jake's Tofu-Turkey Pie, 104
Pad Thai, 129
Tofu Paté with Spring Herbs, 89

TOMATOES
Aunt Stel's Piccalilli, 200
Baked Tomato Spaghetti, 127
Barley and Lentil Soup with
   Swiss Chard, 151
Claudia's Summer Crostini, 118
Debbie's Roasted Tomato Sauce, 193
Dried, 191
Dried Tomato Pesto, 146
Eggplant Bruschetta, 119
Fall Stew, 165
Fried Green Tomatoes, 171
Frozen, 190
Gazpacho, 126
Green Bean Tomato Curry, 136
Kohlrabi and Sungold Tomato
   Salad, 148
Minestrone, 152
Pasta Salad with Tomato and
   Feta Cheese, 122
Pesto and Fresh Tomato Pizza, 186
Ratatouille with Polenta, 166
Real Deal Cream of Tomato Soup, 154
Roasted Tomato Sauce, 192
Summer Season Features, 117
Storage, 204
Tabbouli, 125
Tomatoes Lutèce, 121

TOMATILLOS
Summer Season Features, 117

TURNIPS
Bulgar and Winter Vegetables, 59
Carrot and Turnip Pancakes, 72
Curried Winter Vegetable Soup, 52
Mid-Winter Vegetable Cure, 66
Winter Season Features, 41
Winter Salads, 46

WHEAT BERRIES
Wheat Berry Salad with Fresh Peas, 94
Whole Grain Salads, 207

ZUCCHINI, see also Squash, Summer
Groundwork Organic's Favorite
   Veggie Melt, 131
Mexican Veggie Pot Pie, 132
Minestrone, 152
Ratatouille with Polenta, 166
Zucchini and Basil Pizza, 186

IDEAS, NOTES & RECIPES

IDEAS, NOTES & RECIPES

IDEAS, NOTES & RECIPES